FAMILY REFERENCE

DEALING WITH A DEATH IN THE FAMILY

How to manage the emotional and practical difficulties surrounding a death

Sylvia Murphy

How To Books

British Library Cataloguing in Publication Data
A catalogue record for this book is available from the British Library.

First published in 1997 by How To Books Ltd, 3 Newtec Place,
Magdalen Road, Oxford, OX4 1RE, United Kingdom.
Tel: (01865) 793806. Fax: (01865) 248780.

Note: The material contained in this book is set out in good faith for general
guidance and no liability can be accepted for loss or expense incurred as a
result or relying in particular circumstances on statements made in the book.
The laws and regulations are complex and liable to change, and readers
should check the current position with the relevant authorities before making
personal arrangements.

Produced for How To Books by Deer Park Productions.

Typeset by Anneset, Weston-super-Mare, North Somerset.
Printed and bound by Cromwell Press, Broughton Gifford, Melksham, Wiltshire.

DEALING WITH A DEATH IN THE FAMILY

1. **This book may be kept three weeks. It is to be returned on / before the last date stamped below.**
2. **A fine of ~~~~ ~~~~ ed for every week or ~~~~ ~~~~ ~~~~ le.**

How To Books for Family Reference

Arranging Insurance
Becoming a Father
Buying a Personal Computer
Cash from Your Computer
Choosing a Nursing Home
Choosing a Package Holiday
Dealing with a Death in the Family
Having a Baby
Helping Your Child to Read
How to Apply to an Industrial Tribunal
How to be a Local Councillor
How to be an Effective School Governor
How to Claim State Benefits
How to Lose Weight & Keep Fit
How to Make a Wedding Speech
How to Plan a Wedding
How to Raise Funds & Sponsorship
How to Run a Local Campaign
How to Run a Voluntary Group
How to Survive Divorce
How to Take Care of Your Heart
How to Use the Internet
Making a Complaint
Making a Video
Managing Your Personal Finances
Successful Grandparenting
Successful Single Parenting
Taking in Students
Teaching Someone to Drive
Winning Consumer Competitions

Other titles in preparation

The How To series now contains more than 200 titles in the
following categories:

Business Basics
Family Reference
Jobs and Careers
Living and Working Abroad
Student Handbooks
Successful Writing

Please sent for a free copy of the latest catalogue for full details
(see back cover for address).

Contents

List of Illustrations

Preface

Like most people, I faced the successive deaths of people dear to me with a terrible sense of loneliness and helplessness. There was no guidance as to what could and had to be done except for a string of time-worn conventions and my own very confused and painful feelings. Each time, I found myself thinking that I could have tackled the before and after of the death so much more helpfully, both for the person who had gone and for those left behind with me, if only . . .

But those 'if only' regrets centred on the fact that I had never had the purpose or courage to sit down and talk about forthcoming death, either mine or someone else's.

If only there had been a simple book to tell me what to expect and how to cope with it!

On hearing that I was going to write such a book many friends and acquaintances thought I was being unduly morbid. But I have found the experience far from morbid. My researches have been endlessly interesting, and talking openly with the people who deal with the many aspects of death every day as part of their working lives has been a most refreshing experience.

I would like to thank every one of those people for the patient and helpful way they have answered my many questions, made helpful suggestions and supported me in this enterprise.

Sylvia Murphy

IS THIS YOU?

Parent   Spouse

Partner

Son   Brother

Sister

Daughter   Grandchild

Family friend

Hospital social worker   Hospital administrator

Hospital matron

Nurse   Community leader

Minister of religion

Police officer   Social worker

Counsellor

Funeral director   Hotel manager

College principal

School headteacher   Staff welfare officer

Staff manager

Personnel officer   Office manager

Solicitor

Executor   Nursing home proprietor

Teacher

Rest home manager   Hospice administrator

Hospice matron

Journalist   Military officer

CAB adviser

Trade union representative   Member of Parliament

1
Approaching Death

LEARNING THAT SOMEONE IS DYING

Facing the truth

There is no such thing as an unexpected death. Everyone knows that they and their loved ones have to die at some point. But because it's such an emotionally painful experience for everyone concerned, people try to avoid talking about it by pretending that it won't happen in their family. The result is that most deaths are not very well prepared for.

So when someone close is diagnosed as having a terminal illness most people don't know how to cope with the situation. They find it difficult to discuss the approaching death with doctors or nurses, with other members of the family and, most important of all, with the person who is dying. Yet without these discussions it's impossible to know what to expect or what to do to make the death as easy as possible for everyone concerned.

Asking questions

One of the first things that both the person who is dying and the relatives need to have is accurate information about what to expect. The obvious person to approach for information is the patient's doctor who can at least be expected to have seen it all before. The sort of things people might want to know are:

- How long has the patient left to live?

- Will they be bedridden for that time?

- Will they be in pain?

- Should we tell the patient the truth?

- Who will look after them?

- Will they stay in hospital or come home?

- What can I do to help?

Finding answers

This isn't as easy as asking the questions because often the doctors just don't know, for several reasons:

- The course of every illness is unpredictable and depends on factors such as the general health of the patient before the illness and the person's will to live or to die.

- The same thing can apply to whether the patient will be bedridden, but almost certainly, as they get weaker, they will be less able to get up and move around.

- Most people fear pain more than the death itself. Modern methods of pain control are very good but may make it difficult for the patient to do anything except lie in bed half-asleep. If possible the patient is given the choice between pain and unconsciousness and most people opt for the quiet, pain-free death, but the doctor can't predict this.

- It used to be considered best not to tell a person that they were going to die soon, but nowadays that would be considered a breach of the patient's rights. Just the same, some doctors still find it a very difficult subject to deal with.

- There are more choices than there used to be about where and by whom a dying person is to be nursed, but the doctor doesn't necessarily know all the factors that would affect a decision in any particular family.

- It's very hard for a doctor to know how people can help when the patient is already being well cared for in the medical sense.

To tell or not to tell?

To return for a moment to the difficult subject of telling the truth about dying, it's little wonder sometimes that doctors don't know what to do for the best.

Often it happens that the person who is dying knows in their heart what is coming and is quite resigned to the situation, but will ask the doctor not to tell the rest of the family so as to spare them too much pain.

On the other hand, the family might be well aware that death is near but ask that the truth is kept from the dying person, thinking that this will make it easier for them.

And some people, told that they are dying, refuse to accept the knowledge by blotting it out from their consciousness.

However, studies show that the majority of patients really do want to know what's going on and that honesty is the least painful policy for all concerned. Most doctors and nurses nowadays consider it to be a part of their job to have question and answer sessions with patient and family to help them to face up to the situation.

The Natural Death Centre has even drawn up a provisional Declaration of Rights for the dying and amongst these is the right '... to the extent that I so wish, to be told the truth about my condition and about the purposes of, alternatives to and consequences of, any proposed treatments'. Carers should always bear in mind that it's the patient who is dying, not them. It should be their role to look after them and keep them informed, not to make decisions for them.

They should also bear in mind that some people's religious beliefs will make it important for them to know beforehand that they are going to die.

CARING FOR THE DYING

Who will look after a dying member of the family and where they will go for the best and most appropriate care is often a difficult question and a decision sometimes has to be made very quickly. On the other hand, sometimes there is no choice because the home situation isn't suitable or there's a shortage of hospital or hospice beds.

Where can the patient go?
However much a family may want to do their best, where they live and how well-off they are may limit the choice about where and how to care for a dying person. But, all things being equal, there may be several options. For example:

- at home
- at the home of a relative
- in hospital
- in a hospice
- in a nursing home.

If the first choice turns out to be unsuitable it needn't necessarily be final. Carers shouldn't be afraid to ask that the patient be transferred somewhere else.

Care at home

Sometimes families feel guilty about the idea of sending the patient away at such a time and try to keep them at home even when it's not appropriate. It's better if a decision about home care can be taken with the best interest of the patient in mind and feelings of guilt or obligation pushed into second place.

If the illness permits it, home care of one kind or another is obviously the best option because most people are happier in their own familiar surroundings. However, it may be that there are young children in the home so that the patient won't be able to get enough rest, or there isn't a room where the patient can be alone.

And if the patient is dependent on drugs to control pain and nausea, home can only be considered if it's possible to arrange for a member of the family to give these drugs, or for qualified nursing attendance. Charities such as the Marie Curie Nursing Service or the Macmillan Cancer Relief Fund provide help and advice about professional nursing care for cancer patients in their own homes.

However, where there's only an elderly partner or an overstretched younger member of the family to do the nursing, home care can become very stressful for the patient and the carers.

If for any of the reasons mentioned above the home environment isn't suitable, the patient may prefer to go into a hospital, a nursing home or a hospice.

Care in a hospital

Sometimes, and in some areas of Britain, this is the only option for a patient who can't be at home. But a bed or a side room in a busy hospital ward isn't an ideal place for someone who's dying. For one thing, there is constant clatter, the chatter of voices of nursing staff and visitors. For another, there will be other patients in the ward who expect to get better and go home and the presence of someone near to death can be upsetting for everyone concerned, not least the dying person.

Care in a nursing home

This could be an option for someone able to pay the costs of nursing home care, either from private means or from private health insurance. It's important to understand that there are different kinds of nursing homes. Some are, in fact, small private hospitals with every medical facility, others are little more than residential homes where many old people go to spend their last years. In the latter the nursing staff may not have full facilities to deal with terminally ill patients.

This situation does vary from one establishment to the other and families should make sure they know what can be provided for their relatives.

Hospice care

Nowadays there is, in many areas of Britain, the option of a hospice for a dying patient.

A hospice is a specially-built unit dedicated to the nursing of terminally ill people, where the aim is to provide palliative care – to improve the quality of the life that is left to the patient and to make death as comfortable and dignified as possible.

The staff are specially trained to deal with dying people and their friends and relatives kindly and sympathetically. The atmosphere is deliberately quieter and gentler than in a busy mainstream hospital.

Wherever the patient is cared for it's obviously important that the place be near enough to the family for regular visiting, and that, as far as possible, the patient is satisfied with the choice.

TELLING OTHER PEOPLE

Another difficult decision is whether to tell more distant family members and the patient's circle of friends and acquaintances that the patient is going to die. A family member who is already stressed and upset can find it very difficult to cope with a lot of enquiries from people who are, quite naturally, concerned about the patient. It's even worse to have to make multiple telephone calls to deliver the painful news.

However, people will want to know what's happening and some of them may feel very upset if they learn of the death and weren't told in advance what was expected. They may feel cheated of an opportunity to say goodbye, or simply to express some kind of support. And while someone is sick and still able to make sense of what's going on, flowers and cards often cheer a dull routine.

On the other hand, the last thing that dying people, or their carers, need is visitors constantly coming and going and some people have to be told gently that visiting is too tiring for the patient.

Forming a chain of information

One good way of coping with this situation is to enlist the help of close friends and family members not immediately involved in the patient's care, to form a chain of information through the circle of friends. This can happen when the patient first becomes seriously ill and the news of deterioration can gradually be passed along this chain in a tactful way. Then, when the death actually occurs, everyone will be ready for it and the pain of passing on the news to a lot of people will be taken from the shoulders of those closest to the loss.

SAYING GOODBYE

It's very difficult and painful to decide how and when to say goodbye to someone you love who is dying. If someone is sinking into a coma induced by pain-relieving drugs, it's highly likely that they may not know who is talking to them and touching them for several days before death. Yet saying goodbye when they are conscious and able to understand what you are saying might seem like jumping the gun or preparing to abandon them.

Hospitals and hospices make special arrangements for family members to be near the patient for as long as they want to be. There are residential rooms for visitors who have travelled a long way, or want to be around 24 hours a day, and family members can help the staff in the everyday details of the care of the patient, such as washing and feeding.

Many families feel the need to keep a close vigil and to be present at the death, and this isn't discouraged. However, people are often shocked to discover that by the time death comes it's too late to say goodbye because the patient never regains consciousness.

For this reason, some families prefer the second option of taking their leave early, then going away and placing the patient's final hours or days in the hands of the professionals.

SUPPORTING EACH OTHER

People find it hard to believe how stressed and emotional they become during and immediately after the death of someone close. It may be that the death is seen as a final release from pain and illness but the emotions it releases are just as strong. Bursting into tears unexpectedly is the least of the things that happen.

Common experiences following a death

- poor concentration

- loss of memory

- uncontrollable shaking

- dizzy spells

- inability to sleep

- inability to voice your thoughts

- inability to remember where you are or what you are doing

- inability to make rational decisions.

All this can be very frightening to someone who is used to coping with everyday life without major problems. It's important to remember that these are perfectly normal reactions and even if some of them persist for a while they'll all fade away eventually.

In the meantime it can help if friends, family and work colleagues know about these reactions and give each other support. For example, if possible always make sure there are two of you out and about together and avoid making important decisions connected with your work situation or affecting the rest of someone's life. Sometimes people are so deeply shocked at first that it's not advisable for them to drive.

Unfortunately, the next of kin won't be able to avoid making a lot of the important decisions about the deceased and related family affairs that are dealt with in this book. But working through them together, with time to consider each point carefully, will make things easier to cope with.

CHECKLIST

If you know someone close to you is dying:

1. Don't be afraid to ask questions – get informed and get a picture of what to expect.

2. Don't be afraid to talk about the truth.

3. Find out what the dying person's wishes are – remember it's their death, not yours.

4. Make sure that the patient is getting the best possible care under the circumstances.

5. Make arrangements to keep family and friends informed.

6. Remember that carers suffer stress as well as the patient and don't be frightened by the symptoms of stress.

7. Be mutually supportive with other members of the family circle.

CASE STUDIES

Ralph learns that his wife is dying

Ralph is a retired head teacher in his mid-60s who has been married to Jane, a local government officer, for 30 years. They have three children – John and Peter, who are married and live way from home, and Angela, a student who lives at home. Jane has been feeling unwell for some months and when she is finally persuaded to see a doctor she is diagnosed as having cervical cancer which has spread too far to be curable.

Jane knows that the last stages of her disease will be unpleasant and painful and she decides that the stress of nursing her at home would seriously affect Ralph's health and Angela's studies. She asks to be admitted to a hospice where, because of her private medical insurance, she can have a room of her own. Ralph and Angela visit her every day and she is able to discuss her will and plan her funeral with Ralph. John and Peter bring their families to stay at the hospice to be near her over the weekends. She dies peacefully and without pain, with her family around her.

Isabel pretends that nothing is wrong

Isabel is the wife of Alistair, a Scottish farmer in his early 70s. They have one grown-up son, Ian, who works on the farm and lives with his girlfriend, Anna, in a nearby cottage. Alistair is becoming increas-

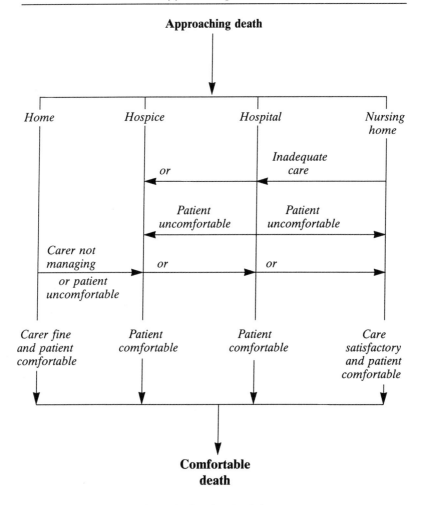

Fig. 1. Caring for the dying.

ingly forgetful about day to day matters and is unable to make the decisions necessary to manage the farm so Ian has more or less taken over and humours him so that he believes he is still in charge.

During the winter Alistair catches bronchitis and the doctor admits him to hospital. While he is there the doctors tell Isabel that they are sure he has Alzheimer's disease and that over the coming months he will become increasingly senile so that it will be difficult for her to look after him at home. She tells them he's just forgetful, and not to interfere, and when he has recovered from the bronchitis he is sent home.

DISCUSSION POINTS

1. Do you want to make sure the patient knows that death is near, but don't know what to say? How can you deal with this?

2. Are you satisfied that the patient is receiving the best possible care? If not, what can you do about it?

3. Would you feel more comfortable if you were able to have a long talk with the doctors or nurses looking after the patient? Have you asked for a time to speak to one of them in private?

4. Have you been annoyed by people who hardly know the patient making unnecessary visits? What can you do to discourage them?

5. Are you feeling too shaky to carry on coping without a break? Who can you turn to for help?

2
Dealing with Sudden Death

DYING SUDDENLY

There may be no such thing as an unexpected death but it would be wrong to give the impression that all deaths can be anticipated and prepared for in calm, rational surroundings. A proportion of deaths occur in traumatic circumstances such as accidents, suicides, murders or cot deaths, or from natural but unforseen causes such as heart attacks or strokes. In these cases there are special procedures to follow involving the police and a Coroner in England, Wales or Northern Ireland, or a Procurator Fiscal in Scotland.

Even something as seemingly simple as falling down the stairs comes into this category. In England and Wales, if the deceased has not been seen by a doctor for the complaint that caused death within the last 14 days, the Coroner has to be informed. The time limit in Northern Ireland is 28 days. In Scotland there is no time limit as long as the doctor is satisfied that the death was from natural causes.

This can all add to the complications of registration and funeral arrangements and, of course, increases the burden of shock or grief for the relatives.

Dealing with an accidental death at home
There are all sorts of ways someone might die by accident in the home. For example:

- electrocution
- falling
- scalding or burning
- bleeding to death from a cut
- choking
- suffocation
- poisoning

- drowning
- cot death.

If someone else is present that person is most likely to call an ambulance, or ask a neighbour to do so, because there might be some hope of saving the victim. If the victim is dead when the ambulance arrives the paramedics will take the body straight to the nearest hospital mortuary. It could be that the family GP will be called to the emergency in which case the GP will make arrangements for the body to be removed.

Finding a body
It could also happen that someone meets with an accidental death when nobody is present. When the body is found the person concerned should call the police and the body will eventually be removed to the mortuary. Anyone finding a dead body shouldn't move the body or disturb anything at the scene until the police and a doctor have arrived and had a look around.

Dealing with a sudden death from natural causes
People do sometimes drop down dead from a heart attack or stroke without prior warning. And old people sometimes fade away in their sleep. Such cases are dealt with in the same way as an accidental death. The first thing to do is to call a doctor.

INFORMING A CORONER OR PROCURATOR FISCAL

In the case of sudden death, whatever the cause, in England and Wales and Northern Ireland a GP or the doctor on duty at the hospital will say that they are unable to issue a Certificate of Cause of Death and they will speak to the Coroner. This doesn't mean they don't know what caused the death, but the law is clear that in those circumstances the Coroner has to be informed.

In Scotland the Procurator Fiscal will be informed by the attending doctor or the police only if there are suspicious circumstances.

Sometimes, of course, nobody will know what has happened until there has been an autopsy (*post mortem* examination) and an inquiry.

As well as accidental or cot deaths, the Coroner or Procurator Fiscal must be informed in the following cases:

- death from an industrial disease

- death in custody (police custody or a prison)

- death while under medical or surgical treatment in hospital.

A Coroner will ask for a formal identification of the body, then have a talk with the doctor concerned in the case. If the doctor is able to say that the cause of death was obviously natural, that the victim has been a patient for some time, that it was known that the victim was ill even if there was no consultation recently, the Coroner is able to agree, then and there, that no autopsy or inquest is necessary and the doctor can issue the Cause of Death Certificate. Then the family can proceed to register the death in the normal way. This actually happens in up to one third of the cases reported to a Coroner.

Moving a body into or out of the country
The Coroner or Procurator Fiscal has to be asked for a certificate if a body is to be moved to a foreign country for a funeral, and informed if one is to be brought in from a foreign country.

For these purposes Scotland, Northern Ireland and England and Wales are all foreign countries to each other.

INVOLVING THE POLICE

Wherever a sudden death takes place the police will visit the next of kin to take statements about the circumstances surrounding the death and arrange for a formal identification of the body. Families are worried when the police call at the house or come to talk to them at the hospital after a death. They fear that they may be suspected of a crime it is obvious they haven't committed and this can only add to their distress in what is already a horrible situation.

But the police involvement here is a formality, which isn't to say that it isn't important. Identification is a legal requirement and the statements made at the time may have to be used in evidence at an inquest in England, Wales and Northern Ireland, or a fatal accident enquiry (FAI) in Scotland.

NEEDING AN AUTOPSY

When is an autopsy necessary?
If the Coroner or Procurator Fiscal agrees that the doctor doesn't know enough about the circumstances to issue a certificate, further enquiries will be made and an autopsy will be ordered. This will be

carried out without delay at the nearest large hospital by a consultant pathologist. If a crime is suspected the autopsy will be carried out by a forensic pathologist, most probably in a police mortuary.

Also, if the next of kin have any suspicions of their own they have the right to ask for an independent autopsy, even after one has been carried out on behalf of the authorities.

Some people are upset to think of the body of their loved one being subjected to this kind of examination. Even worse, it is against the religious beliefs of some people. However, the law makes no concessions in these cases and must be accepted by everyone because its purpose is to deal fairly with every case of sudden or accidental death.

Finding no suspicious circumstances

If the autopsy reveals beyond doubt that the cause of death was natural, not accidental, and there is no suspicion that a crime has been committed, there will be no further investigation. When the pathologist's report has been received the Coroner or Procurator Fiscal will issue the Cause of Death Certificate. In some cases the next of kin will have to collect the certificate, in some cases it will be sent straight to the registrar.

Then the death can be registered in the normal way and the body released for burial or cremation.

HOLDING AN INQUEST/INQUIRY

Following the pathologist's report, a Coroner or Procurator Fiscal will order an inquest or a fatal accident inquiry if:

- the cause of death is still uncertain

- the circumstances leading up to the death are uncertain

- there is suspicion that a crime has been committed

- there is evidence that the death was suicide

- the death was accidental or violent and there is likelihood of a manslaughter case

- the death was accidental and there is likelihood of an insurance claim

- the death was caused by industrial injury, because of possible claims for compensation

- the death was caused during medical or surgical treatment, because of possible claims and/or prosecutions

- the death was in custody, because of pending investigations and/or claims.

An inquest or inquiry can also be held in a case where there is no body – for example, someone has gone missing overboard from a boat or disappeared climbing or been in the path of an avalanche or a severe storm. In that case the Coroner or Procurator Fiscal must have permission from the Home or Scottish Office, and this will only be granted if a reasonable length of time has elapsed.

Informing the next of kin

The police or Coroner's officer should explain to the next of kin the reasons why an inquest is being held and keep them fully informed at all times. In Scotland the Procurator Fiscal will be responsible for passing on the necessary information.

Just as with an autopsy, the next of kin has no option to refuse but they do have a right to know what is happening. And if they think the case has been mishandled they can apply for a Judicial Review to challenge the findings of the inquest or inquiry.

What happens at an inquest/inquiry?

An inquest is a lawfully constituted court but it is not a court of law. Its purpose is to establish the identity of the deceased and what has happened. It can issue a verdict as to cause of death but it can't apportion guilt or blame to people concerned with the death. The court may take place in a special Coroner's court room, it may be in a less formal magistrates' court, it may be set up in a room in the nearest municipal buildings. At one time there used to be a jury at all inquests but things have been simplified now. An individual Coroner can call a jury of eight or ten people or can do without. The only circumstances in which a jury is compulsory is when a death has occurred in custody or as a result of an accident at work.

In Scotland the inquiry is held in a local sheriff's court. There the Procurator Fiscal examines the witnesses but the Sheriff presides and arrives at the verdict.

Just as in any other court or inquiry, witnesses will be called to give evidence of identification and to give their versions of the circumstances surrounding the death. It is possible for people who are unable to attend to submit evidence by written statement.

The next of kin are allowed to question witnesses and are strongly advised to have a solicitor present in case there should be any later legal proceedings or insurance claims.

Giving a verdict

In a straightforward case, when the Coroner or Sheriff is satisfied that all the evidence has been presented and the case is clear there will be a 'summing up' and a verdict will be given. It could be:

- natural causes

- accidental death – caused by an unavoidable set of circumstances, not the fault of the dead person

- unlawful killing – which could be murder or manslaughter and would be the result of a criminal investigation

- suicide – caused by the victim's own hand

- misadventure – due to an accident caused by a deliberate act which could have been the fault of the dead person

- an open verdict – when the cause is not clear and may never be fully known, but the inquest can be reopened with further evidence.

Adjourning an inquest

Sometimes, as in the case of a road traffic or industrial accident, it may take the police or accident investigator some weeks or months to conclude their enquiries. But if the pathologist no longer needs the body for examination it can be released for a funeral once the inquest or inquiry is opened, formal identification is taken and the proceedings then adjourned. Then a cremation certificate or a burial order will be issued. When the accident investigation is finally complete the inquest or inquiry will continue and a verdict will be given, after which a full Certificate of Cause of Death will be issued and the death can be properly registered.

The Coroner can also issue an Interim Death Certificate in cases where the next of kin needs to prove the death to release funds from a bank or building society.

However, if there is any suspicion that the death might have been due to murder or manslaughter the body cannot be released even after the inquest has been opened. This is because if there is a subsequent criminal trial the defence lawyers have the right to demand another *post mortem*. This can hold up the funeral for a long time and there is nothing that can be done about it.

If it's known that there has been foul play but no arrest is made the body will be released after a 'decent interval'.

DONATING ORGANS

Being a donor for transplant surgery

Most of the major organs of the body can now be successfully transplanted and there are thousands of people waiting for donated organs so that they can live a normal life. But organs can only be used if they are removed fairly quickly from the dead body.

Unfortunately this means that, just to add to all the distress, a family bereaved by sudden death in a hospital will certainly be asked whether the organs can be removed for transplant surgery. It's a help to the hospital staff if a victim has been carrying a donor card because then, technically, next of kin don't have to be asked. However, if they are around they will usually be consulted as a matter of courtesy.

If there is no donor card and permission is refused it is illegal for a doctor to remove any organ for transplant surgery.

Donating a body for medical research

If a person's body has been accepted for medical research (see Chapter 10), then an immediate funeral isn't possible and a memorial service is arranged instead. Later, when the body has been finished with, the hospital will usually pay for a funeral.

DEALING WITH THE STRESS

Suffering post-traumatic stress

Anyone who has been involved with a sudden death, whether as a witness, as the person who finds the body or as the next of kin, has a special kind of shock to deal with that compounds the ordinary distress of bereavement. It's referred to as post-traumatic stress. Carers, medical practitioners, police personnel, coroners and counsellors should know about this and should behave accordingly towards the people they are dealing with.

Many people cope with all forms of post-traumatic stress without help and appear to make a rapid and complete recovery and return to normal life. Many never seem able to recover. Some seem to recover and the experience stress-related breakdowns years afterwards. It's important to remember that extreme reactions are normal and are increasingly recognised as a genuine form of illness.

Anyone suffering stress from any of these causes will be able to get help from their GP or from a bereavement counsellor, as discussed in Chapter 9.

CHECKLIST

If someone close to you dies suddenly:

1. Don't be alarmed if the police begin to ask questions.

2. Don't be alarmed if you are told a Coroner or Procurator Fiscal must be informed.

3. Remember that any inquires are aimed at establishing the truth, not making life difficult for you and your family.

4. Remember that you may have to wait some time before you can arrange the funeral.

5. Remember that you have a right to be kept informed about what is happening.

6. Remember that you have a right to be represented at any inquiry.

7. Don't be too upset if you are asked by the hospital if they can remove organs for transplant – this is to help other people.

8. Don't be afraid to ask for help when you or a member of your family suffer from post-traumatic stress.

CASE STUDIES

Alistair falls down the stairs

Not long after Alistair has been discharged from hospital, Isabel is woken one night by a terrible crash. She finds Alistair at the bottom of the stairs. She can't move him or revive him and she telephones her son, then the doctor. The doctor says Alistair is dead and that he must inform the Procurator Fiscal. Later, Isabel and Ian are worried to hear that there will be an autopsy and things are made worse when the police come round to ask questions.

The autopsy reveals multiple injuries, including a blow to the head and a broken neck, either of which could have killed Alistair. It also confirms Alzheimer's disease. At the inquiry the Sheriff decides that Isabel is too frail to have caused death by hitting Alistair or pushing him down the stairs, and he brings a verdict of accidental death.

Jaswant meets with an accident

Jaswant, wife of Ram, who runs a family-owned grocery shop, is walking with her neighbour to meet their children from school. She is so busy talking that she steps off the pavement in front of a motorcycle and is seriously injured. She is taken by ambulance to the nearest hospital casualty department where Ram soon arrives with his mother and mother-in-law, closely followed by his father, Amrit, who is a Sikh community leader.

Within a couple of hours Jaswant dies of her injuries. The family are asked whether any of her organs can be used for transplant surgery and they refuse because it's against their cultural beliefs to cut up the dead body. They are shocked to be told that the Coroner must be informed and there must be an autopsy to establish the exact cause of death, followed by an inquest. This is even more upsetting because according to Sikh custom funerals must take place within 24 hours of the death. Amrit explains to Ram that they must accept the law, and he will make sure everything is done as correctly as is possible in the circumstances.

DISCUSSION POINTS

1. Would you feel victimised if police officers called at your house to make inquiries after a member of your family met with an accident? What can you do about this?

2. Are you able to say with confidence that your next of kin would be willing to donate organs after death?

3. How would you expect to find out the date of an inquest or inquiry to be held about the death of your next of kin?

4. What would you be able to do if you disagreed with the verdict of an inquest or inquiry?

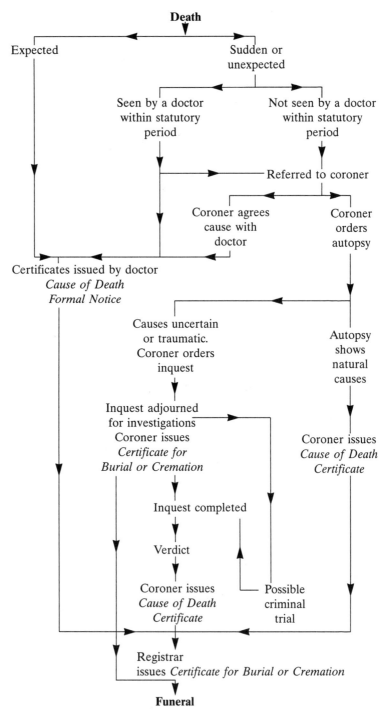

Fig. 2. Dealing with a death – England and Wales. (Scotland and Northern Ireland have similar but slightly different procedures.)

3
Doing the Paperwork

REGISTERING A DEATH

Unless the matter is in the hands of a Coroner or Procurator Fiscal the death must be registered within five days in England and Wales and Northern Ireland, eight days in Scotland.

From April 1997 in England and Wales the death may be registered in any register office. In Scotland or Northern Ireland the registration can take place either where the person lived or where the death happened if this is a different place, whichever is more convenient.

Even in the most straightforward case there are several stages to go through and at the time it seems as though dying is one of the most complicated things that happens to anyone. Unfortunately the dead person isn't the one who is required to do this paperwork. Most of it falls to the next of kin who, in many cases, is the one suffering most deeply from the shock of bereavement and therefore in the worst possible state to deal with everything.

The officials involved in processing this paperwork are generally well aware of the problems the next of kin will be facing. However, they have a job to do and have to get on with it. Anyone suffering from the first shock of bereavement and finding themselves in the situation of having to register a death would be well advised, if at all possible, to ask a trusted friend or relative to accompany them.

The address of the nearest Registrar will be found in the local telephone directory under R for Registration of Births, Deaths and Marriages, though normally the hospital or doctor will be able to tell the next of kin where to go. Some register offices operate an appointment system, some don't, and opening hours vary from place to place. So a preliminary telephone call to find out the local situation can save time and a wasted journey.

Who can register a death?

Only certain people can act as 'informants' – in other words able to register the death.

If the person died at home or in a public institution such as hospital, hospice, prison, old people's home etc, the death can be registered by:

- a relative of the deceased who was present at the death

- a relative of the deceased not present at the death but in attendance during the last illness

- a relative residing in the sub-district where the death occurred

- some other person present at the death

- the governor, master, matron, superintendent or other officer of a public institution if he or she knew of the death happening

- any inmate of a public institution if he or she knew of the death happening

- the person causing the disposal of the body (this could be an official representative of the family, such as a solicitor).

If the person died out of doors, or the body was found later, the death can be registered by:

- any relative of the deceased who knows the facts required by the Registrar

- any person present at the death

- any person who found the body

- any person in charge of the body

- the person causing the disposal of the body.

ESTABLISHING THE FACTS

The registration processes following a death have two aims:

1. To establish the cause of death.

2. To establish the identity of the person who has died.

Only when both of these have been done can the body be released for burial or cremation.

Establishing cause of death

The medical certificates are the documents that officially establish the cause of the death. There are different certification procedures for different circumstances.

If the deceased has been in the care of a doctor within the last 14 days in England and Wales, 28 days in Northern Ireland, for the condition that caused the death, the attending doctor will issue:

• a certificate stating the cause of death

• a formal notice that the doctor has signed the medical certificate and telling you how to register the death.

These certificates will also be issued if the doctor hasn't treated the patient within the qualifying periods, but the Coroner is satisfied that the death was due to natural causes.

In Scotland there is no qualifying period for treatment if the doctor is certain the death was due to natural causes.

If there is an autopsy to find out the cause of death, but the Coroner or Procurator Fiscal then decides that no inquest is necessary, a Cause of Death Certificate will then be issued by the Coroner or the Procurator's office. If the body is to be cremated a certificate for cremation will also be issued.

If there has to be an inquest but the body is no longer required, the Coroner or Sheriff will open the inquest for identification and then adjourn it and a burial order or cremation certificate will be issued so that a funeral can take place. After the final verdict of the court or inquiry a form will be sent to the Registrar and the death can be officially registered.

Refusing registration

If the Registrar comes upon anything during the course of the registration interview that makes him or her think that the cause of death may not be what is stated on the doctor's certificate, the registrar will refuse to complete the registration and inform the Coroner that further investigation is needed.

For example, the Certificate might say that the cause of death was a heart attack but it might be mentioned in the course of conversation that the deceased fell down stairs a few hours before dying, which wasn't brought to the doctor's attention at the time.

Establishing the identity of the deceased

The informant must take everything necessary to establish the identity of the deceased beyond doubt and to prove the death has taken place so that the Registrar can record that the deceased is no longer living.

What does the informant need?

The informant must take the Medical Cause of Death Certificate issued by the doctor or the Cause of Death form issued by the Coroner. The cause of death stated on these forms will be couched in complicated medical language that many people won't be able to understand. Anyone who is puzzled by these terms should ask the doctor or Coroner's officer what they mean in everyday language.

The informant should also take, if possible:

• the birth and marriage certificates of the deceased

• details of any life insurance policies

• the deceased's medical card

• any pension or allowance book.

What will the Registrar want to know?

In addition to the documents above the Registrar will want to know:

• the date and place of the death

• the last usual address of the deceased

- first names and surname (and maiden name where relevant) of the deceased

- whether the deceased was known by any other names

- the date and place of birth of the deceased

- the occupation of the deceased and the name and occupation of their spouse or previous spouse(s)

- the date of birth of any surviving widow or widower

- whether the deceased was getting any pension or allowance from public funds.

What does the Registrar do?

When all these details have been collected the Registrar makes a formal entry in the Registrar of Deaths. Some people worry if they later discover that they have made some mistake in the background details (for example, information about past spouses or places and dates of marriages may not always be readily available). The Registrar is trying to establish the identity of the deceased in the most complete way possible and any genuine error doesn't make the whole process invalid.

GETTING A DEATH CERTIFICATE

What does the Registrar give the informant?

Unless the Coroner has already issued an Order for Burial or a Certificate for Cremation, the Registrar will give the next of kin a Certificate for Burial or Cremation, known as the Green Form (Figure 3) which the funeral director, crematorium director or burial ground superintendent must have before a funeral can take place. In Scotland this is called a Certificate of Registration of Death.

The Registrar will also issue a Certificate of Registration of Death. This is only for the Social Security Office. If any of the information on the back of that certificate applies to the family of the deceased, fill it in and send it off. By law the Registrar has to inform any government departments from whom the deceased may have been receiving a pension (for example doctors, teachers, armed forces *etc*).

There will also be leaflets about widow's benefits and pensions, if appropriate.

Unless this document is delivered intact to the person mentioned overleaf, the burial or cremation may be delayed.

DIS
23 750457

PART B

Births and Deaths Registration Act 1953, S. 24 (1)

CERTIFICATE FOR BURIAL OR CREMATION (Issued *after* registration)

I, the undersigned registrar, do hereby certify that the death of

JANE SANDERS

aged 61 .... who died on 20th SEPTEMBER 199X

at ST. STEPHENS HOSPICE .. ANYTOWN. 000.

.... has been duly registered by me at Entry No. 000.

Witness my hand this 21ST .... day of SEPTEMBER 19 9X

A.Z. SMITH .... (Registrar of Births and Deaths)

Registration District .... Sub-district ....

CERTIFICATE FOR BURIAL (Issued *before* registration)
(This Certificate is not available for purposes of Cremation)

I, the undersigned registrar, do hereby certify that the death of

aged ....

at .... who died on ....

.... has been duly notified to me.

Witness my hand this .... day of .... 19 ....

.... (Registrar of Births and Deaths)

Registration District .... Sub-district ....

IMPORTANT.—If it is intended to remove the body out of England and Wales for burial, etc., notice must be given to the Coroner in advance of the intended removal. A form for giving notice may be obtained from the Registrar giving this certificate. If the Death has not already been registered it must be registered within 14 days of the date on which it took place by a relative of the deceased or one of the persons required by law to give information for the purpose.

DIS
23 750457

PART C

NOTIFICATION OF BURIAL OR CREMATION (see back).

Births and Deaths Registration Act 1926, S.3(1) [Form prescribed by the Registration of Births and Deaths Regulations 1987].

This is to notify that the body of

....

deceased, who died on ....

at ....

was buried/cremated* on ....

at ....

(Signature) ....

on behalf of ....

....

Date ....

*Strike out whichever does not apply.

Fig. 3. The 'Green Form' – Registrar's certificate for burial or cremation, side 1.

38

D. Cert.
R.B.D.

CAUTION - It is an offence to falsify a certificate or to make or knowingly use a false certificate or a copy of a false certificate intending it to be accepted as genuine to the prejudice of any person, or to possess a certificate knowing it to be false without lawful authority.

CERTIFIED COPY
Pursuant to the Births and

OF AN ENTRY
Deaths Registration Act 1953

DEATH	Entry Number **000**

Registration District
Sub-district

Administrative area

1. Date and place of death

ST. STEPHEN'S HOSPICE, ANYTOWN.   20 SEPT. 199X

2. Name and surname

JANE SANDERS

3. Sex FEMALE

4. Maiden surname of woman who has married   GREEN

5. Date and place of birth

6TH FEBRUARY 1934   SOMETOWN, ENGLAND

6. Occupation and usual address

LOCAL GOVERNMENT OFFICER (RETIRED)
2, THE GREEN, ANYTOWN.

7. (a) Name and surname of informant

RALPH SANDERS

(b) Qualification

HUSBAND

(c) Usual address

2, THE GREEN, ANYTOWN

8. Cause of death

METASTATIC CARCINOMA

9. I certify that the particulars given by me above are true to the best of my knowledge and belief.

R. Sanders

Signature of informant

10. Date of registration

21st SEPTEMBER 199X

11. Signature of registrar

A.Z. SMITH

Certified to be a true copy of an entry in a register in my custody.

.... Registrar   .... Date

Fig. 4. Certified copy of an entry in the Register of Deaths (death certificate).

Asking for a death certificate

The last document, which is what most people mean when they refer to a 'Death Certificate', is a formal copy of the entry in the Register (Figure 4). Unlike the other documents listed above it isn't issued as a matter of course. The informant has to ask for it, and it has to be paid for. At the present time (1996) the cost is £2.50 per copy at the time of registration, but it costs more to get copies at a later date. This is the only charge that the Registrar will make.

This copy certificate will be required for any of the business that is done after death concerning the financial affairs of the deceased. It will also be required by the widow or widower if they want to remarry.

Some offices and organisations will accept photocopies of the certificate, most of them will return it after they have seen it and made a note of its existence. However, it's still a good idea to have plenty of copies because this will speed things up.

Some Registrars' offices will issue these copies immediately, some will post them within a few days.

REGISTERING A STILLBIRTH OR NEONATAL DEATH

There are slightly different procedures for registering a stillbirth, which is defined as an infant born dead after the 24th week of pregnancy. The birth must be registered within 21 days and the Registrar will need a Certificate of Stillbirth signed by the attending doctor or midwife. If neither of these were present the Registrar will give the parent(s) a form to complete.

The Registrar will then issue a Certificate for Burial or Cremation and a Certificate of Registration of a stillbirth.

It is possible to have a stillborn baby registered with a first name, which the parents often request.

A neonatal death, which is a death that happens within 28 days of birth, has to have separate registrations of birth and death in the normal way, but the two can be done at the same time.

CHECKLIST

If you have to register the death of someone in your family:

1. Check the correct procedure with the police, Coroner or Procurator Fiscal if any of them have been involved.

2. If the death has been straightforward, make sure the doctor gives you the Certificate of Cause of Death and a Formal Notice.

3. Telephone the Registrar's office to find out about opening times and whether you can make an appointment.

4. Write down in advance all the information the registrar will need.

5. Make sure you have all the documents that the Registrar will want to see.

6. Count up in advance the number of copies of the Death Certificate you will need and make sure you have enough money to pay for them.

7. Make sure you know which of the forms you will need from the Registrar to arrange the funeral.

CASE STUDIES

Ralph has everything organised

The doctor in the hospice issued the Certificate of Cause of Death and the Formal Notice on the same day as Jane's death and Ralph is able to make an appointment to see the Registrar the following day. He has all the papers he needs in his desk so there are no problems looking for things. Although he feels quite calm about everything, Angela comes with him and a neighbour offers to drive them in case either of them suffer any stress reaction.

Isabel finds a muddle

As soon as the inquiry is over the Procurator Fiscal's office informs Isabel that the Registrar has been informed of the outcome of the inquiry and she can now register the death. Ian makes an appointment and goes to pick up his mother to take her to the Registrar's office. He finds her searching for birth and marriage certificates amongst a disorganised mass of papers, deeds and farm accounts that have accumulated over the years. Eventually they have to go without these papers, but the death can still be registered and they come away with the certificates they need to arrange a funeral and for Isabel to claim her widow's benefits and pension.

Ram is allowed to arrange Jawsant's funeral

Ram is told that the police enquiries into the accident that killed Jaswant may take some time as there were several witnesses, all of whom have to be interviewed. The Coroner is aware of the need for the funeral to take place as quickly as possible so the day after the autopsy the inquest is opened for formal identification of the body and then adjourned. As the body is not needed for any further examination the Coroner is then able to issue a cremation certificate so that the funeral arrangements can go ahead. Ram and Amrit collect the certificate from the Coroner's office, hurry to the crematorium where they make all the necessary arrangements and book a time the following day. This has to be after the normal working hours, for which they pay extra.

DISCUSSION POINTS

1. Do you know what paperwork is essential to register a death and where to find it?

2. What is the Registrar trying to establish during the registration process?

3. Why might a Registrar refuse to complete a registration?

4
Organising the Funeral

MAKING DECISIONS

Thinking about the deceased

One of the difficulties about arranging a funeral is that there is so much to do, just at a time when the next of kin really wants to shut themselves away and grieve, or try to carry on with their lives as normal. So the temptation is to get it out of the way as quickly and easily as possible. It's as well to remember that this is the only funeral the deceased will have and it's worth taking the trouble to give them the best deal available.

A funeral has several purposes:

1. To dispose of the dead body.

2. To commemorate the life of the dead person.

3. To formalise the mourning process.

The formalities and rituals of funerals are designed to take all these into account but they are only guidelines. Unlike a wedding, which has to follow a certain formula, there is no law about funerals and there is enormous choice about how they can be organised.

Avoiding problems

There are a number of decisions about a funeral have to be made at short notice by the next of kin. When a death has been prepared for, the details of the funeral may already have been discussed within a family (see Chapter 10) and the important decisions made beforehand, taking the wishes of the deceased into account.

When the death happens suddenly it's obviously more difficult for the next of kin who have to make the arrangements, especially if the timing is dictated by the process of the law.

Considering the options

The sort of decisions that have to be made are:

- how much money to spend

- whether to bury or to cremate

- whether to engage a funeral director or do most of the work within the family

- what style of coffin and lining to choose

- whether to have the deceased laid out in a shroud or in their own clothes

- if there is to be a cremation, what will happen to the cremated remains (the ashes)

- whether to have a religious service or a humanist or non-religious ceremony

- whether there is to be a service in church or some other religious centre or only at the crematorium or burial ground

- who to ask to conduct the service or ceremony

- what music and readings to have, if any, and who is to do the playing or reading

- whether to allow flowers or to ask people to give donations to charity

- whether the funeral ceremony is for close family only or for anyone who wants to attend

- whether to offer refreshments afterwards to family and friends

- who to inform directly and whether to put a notice in the local newspaper.

With some religious and cultural groups there is no choice about such details as burying or cremating, the kind of ceremony that will take place and who will conduct it, or how the body is to be laid out.

But any family belonging to one of the many Christian churches, or not having religious beliefs at all, has to think about all these details. It's hardly surprising that many families end up arguing over a funeral, especially families that have been split by divorce and/or remarriage. One part of the family may want to exclude another part from the proceedings, or there may be jealousy as to who is to be responsible for organising the funeral, or acting as host/hostess for any refreshments provided afterwards.

If the next of kin find that the deceased has made all the plans in advance, as more and more people are doing nowadays, there can be nothing but a big sigh of relief all round.

USING A FUNERAL DIRECTOR

Taking advantage of professional experience
It makes sense, in view of all that has to be thought about and done, to turn to a funeral director in this situation, and that's what most families do. There are alternatives, which are discussed in the next chapter, but there's a lot to be said for using the services of a professional who knows about all the requirements and is in the best position to make sure everything runs smoothly.

Checking on standards
It's best to be aware that funeral directing is an unregulated profession, which means that at present there are no legal requirements for entry. Anyone with the necessary capital can set up in the business. There is a National Association of Funeral Directors that regulates standards and offers optional qualifications, but it isn't compulsory for funeral directors to belong to this.

There is also a Funeral Ombudsman Scheme, set up by the Co-operative Funeral movement in April 1994, to which members of the public can complain if they feel they haven't received the service they expected, but the Ombudsman can only investigate funeral directors who are members of the Scheme and, once again, this isn't compulsory.

Shopping around
All this means that, as things stand at present, there can be a wide range of quality and service provided by a funeral director. The

majority do an excellent job to very high standards, but there is the occasional time when the public gets a poor deal.

Normally if people want to buy a service or product they automatically shop around for the best price. The problem with funerals is that the doctor or hospital may organise a funeral director to remove the body, giving the impression that there is little choice in the matter. Or a funeral director contacted on the phone through the *Yellow Pages* will offer to come round to the home of the next of kin and the impression will be that they have already taken over the arrangements. Ninety-seven per cent of all families use the services of the first funeral director they consult.

In fact, unless pre-paid funeral insurance has already been paid that specifies the use of certain companies, there is nothing to prevent the next of kin from shopping around and getting details and quotations from a number of directors, whether the family go to the director's office or the director visits the home.

CREMATING OR BURYING

Thinking about the pros and cons
When the people responsible for arranging the funeral approach a funeral director the first thing that will be asked is whether a cremation or a burial is wanted. It's worth looking at some of the reasons why people might choose cremation or burial.

Choosing cremation

Burning dead bodies
Cremation has only come into general use as a method of disposing of a body since the 1930s. By the 1980s there were more than twice as many cremations as burials and the gap is still widening. It has to be remembered that the number of cremations does depend on the availability of crematoria, which not only have to be built but also have to be upgraded to comply with ever more stringent environmental regulations.

There are three factors behind this growth in the number of cremations:

1. Public health and hygiene: the first cremations took place in Victorian times because of the dreadful smell caused in some churches by rotting corpses and the fear that over-used graveyards in the middle of residential areas could present a public health hazard.

2. Shortage of land: there is such pressure of population on land in
   Britain that if all the people who died were buried, every grave
   would have to be reused time and time again and a lot of extra
   land would have to be designated as burial grounds. Many people
   think that it's better to save the land we have for the use of the
   living.

3. Distaste for the idea of a rotting corpse: in some countries, such
   as the USA, people go to great lengths to make sure the coffin
   and the corpse it contains rot as slowly as possible. In Britain we
   tend to accept the idea that within a few years both will rot away
   six feet underground and will be eaten by worms and other organ-
   isms. However, some people find this idea very distasteful and prefer the quick disposal of a cremation.

There are stories that coffins wait for days for cremation after the
funeral is over. In fact on most occasions the coffin goes straight into
the cremator. Even if there is some hold-up the Code of Cremation
Practice requires the cremation to take place on the same day as the
funeral.

Many crematoria now incorporate a viewing room where the
mourners can actually watch the coffin being committed to the cremator. Safety regulations usually prevent the relatives doing this job
themselves even if they want to.

Disposing of the cremated remains
Another thing that makes cremation more attractive for many
people is that they have a much wider choice of what to do with
the cremated remains (which is how the crematorium authorities
refer to what we normally call the 'ashes') than of what to do with a
body.

Although permission has to be granted to scatter these remains in
a churchyard or any public ground, there is no reason why they can't
be scattered at sea, in a private garden or in some beauty spot without anyone knowing anything about it other than the next of kin. Or
the remains can be scattered or buried in a garden of remembrance
run by the crematorium or by a funeral director, with a memorial
plaque or a plant for permanent commemoration.

Choosing burial

Burying the dead
Burial is the traditional Christian, Jewish or Muslim way of disposing of a body.

This has been encouraged in Britain by the Christian belief in the resurrection of the body. It's difficult to get around the logical conclusion that if there is no body there can be no resurrection and the soul will have nowhere to go. Even after the idea of resurrection was declared to be an ideology rather than a physical fact, and after most British people ceased to think of themselves as Christians, the idea of burying bodies continued to be part of our culture because that's the way it has always been done.

A lot of people prefer the option of burial for several reasons:

1. They live (and die) in areas where there is no crematorium and it would be expensive to transport the body and the mourners specially for a cremation if it isn't strictly necessary.

2. They believe that the rotting process is nature's way of dealing with the dead and we shouldn't interfere with that.

3. A crematorium emits smoke and dust and sometimes unpleasant smells which can pollute the atmosphere and affect the quality of life of people living nearby. Although the regulations are being tightened up to reduce this nuisance it is a fact that cremation is not quite as clean a process as it seems at first.

4. Some people find the idea of their body or that of their loved one being burned very distasteful.

5. At a burial the mourners can see the coffin going into the ground and symbolically start the covering process by throwing in their handful of earth. At a crematorium all they see is a curtain closing or the coffin sliding into another department, and they know that strangers are then going to do something else to it. The mourners can leave a crematorium with the feeling that something has been left unresolved.

SETTING A DATE

Co-ordinating the officials

Once the decisions have been made about what kind of funeral it is to be, the date and time must be settled.

Only in exceptional circumstances can funerals or cremations be arranged at weekends, and then overtime will be charged.

Most funeral directors can handle more than one funeral a day but appointments have also to be made with the crematorium or burial superintendent and any Minister of Religion who is to be involved.

The funeral director will be able to co-ordinate these people quite quickly by telephone either from the family home or from his or her office.

Consulting the family

The close family members will probably not be too worried about one day this way or that, but there may be relatives who have to travel a long distance and depend on public transport timetables. If they have been consulted beforehand and the people making the arrangements already have some idea of what will be convenient to everyone, the decision can be made that much more quickly.

LETTING PEOPLE KNOW

Once the date, time and place have been decided, family and friends have to be informed. Leaving anyone out by mistake or on purpose can cause a lot of unnecessary grief and offence.

Informing the immediate family

Normally the person who is organising the funeral informs the immediate family about the arrangements by telephone. It's important that the person doing this gets over all the facts first time about where people are expected to go and at what time, and what arrangements have been made for cars, either formal cars from the funeral director or informal arrangements within the family. Wishes about flowers should also be passed on at this stage.

Nothing is worse than for grieving people all keyed up for the ordeal of a funeral to end up at the wrong place or be unsure about how they will be able to travel.

Because it's better to get it right first time, it's a good idea to write everything down clearly before making the first phone call.

Informing other relatives

If there is a large family to be informed it's a good idea to let other members take responsibility for those closest to them, either through family connections or geography. If nothing else, it makes them repeat the arrangements to other people and at that stage any uncertainties come to light and can be dealt with before the day.

Informing friends

Many people will have a wide circle of friends and neighbours who will want to know about the funeral so that even if it's not possible or appropriate for them to go they can send flowers or make a memorial donation to charity if they want to. Donations are normally sent to the funeral director, who will eventually give a list to the family so that people can be thanked.

If an information network was organised during the last illness of the deceased, this can be brought into use again to pass around news of the funeral arrangements.

Putting an announcement in the newspaper

One way of making sure everyone knows about funeral arrangements is to put an announcement in the local newspaper. If this is to be done, friends and neighbours can be told to keep a look out for it when they are told about the death. It's a useful method of passing on information in the case of someone who was well known in the area, when possible contacts from the past might otherwise miss out on the news. But it's not done by every family.

PROVIDING REFRESHMENTS

The 'funeral tea' or 'wake' is a fixed tradition in some circles. Most people who plan their own funerals like to arrange for their family and friends to have a bit of a get together after the funeral. There is no doubt that this kind of event after the ordeal of the funeral serves many purposes:

- People can talk openly about the deceased and their feelings about the death. For many of them this will be an important part of the grieving process.

- People who have travelled a long way to the funeral will need to eat and drink.

- People who haven't met for years can get together and swap memories and telephone numbers.

- People who have felt grim and burdened can begin to enjoy themselves again and actually have a laugh.

- People can have a good cry too.

Certain religious groups have rules laid down about exactly how long this hospitality should go on, what is to be eaten and who is to provide the food and drink. However, the kind of provision made by a secular family is entirely up to them. It may be:

- a reception in a hotel, restaurant or public house

- a meal or reception in the home of the deceased or a close relative

- a meal or reception in the local village hall or church hall

- a meal or reception in a club of which the deceased was a member

- a quick cup of tea and piece of cake in the home of the deceased or a close relative

- nothing.

But apart from this last being a discourtesy to mourners, funerals where nothing is provided have probably missed out one of the most important functions of the funeral – to say goodbye to the deceased and see the living on their way to pick up the threads of life again.

CHECKLIST

1. There are a lot of important decisions to make about the way a funeral is to be arranged.

2. Remember, it's the only funeral the deceased will ever have, so it's up to the next of kin to make it as good as possible.

3. A funeral director knows how to arrange the formalities and makes things easier for the family.

4. Before you go to a funeral director, make a list of the points you want to ask about.

5. There is no reason why you can't get quotations from a number of funeral directors.

6. Get help from friends and family to pass on information about the funeral arrangements and try not to leave anyone out.

CASE STUDIES

Alistair has a traditional send-off

Isabel goes with Ian to the funeral director in the nearest town and they arrange for Alistair to be buried in the cemetery of the church where they were married and the children were baptised. They are able to purchase a double plot so that Isabel can eventually be buried there as well. They order a medium-priced coffin, and a funeral car for the family. The funeral director makes all the arrangements, including putting notices in the local newspaper. Anna and Isabel work hard the day before the funeral to provide a generous funeral tea in the farmhouse. Isabel finds that she almost enjoys this social occasion, which is the first time for years that she has entertained her friends and neighbours at her home.

DISCUSSION POINTS

1. Do you have any idea of the kind of funerals members of your family would like to have? If not, what can you do about this?

2. Do you have any preference between burial and cremation? How can you find out more about these options?

3. How can you best arrange a funeral at a convenient time for all those who want to attend?

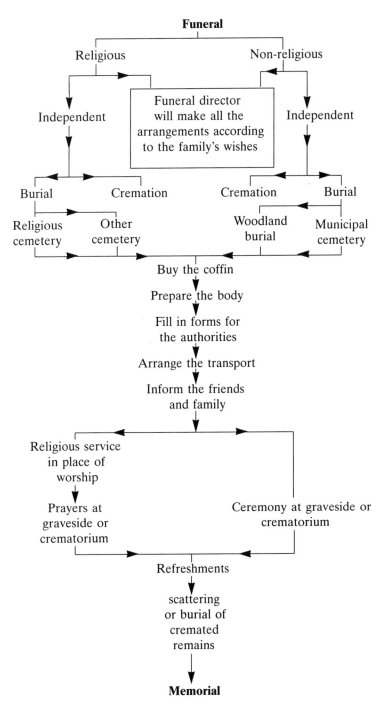

Fig. 5. Organising a funeral.

5
Making Alternative Funeral Arrangements

BELONGING TO NON-CHRISTIAN RELIGIONS

Following religious preferences

Britain is a free country as far as religious worship goes and many religions other than Christianity are represented in our society. Whatever religion the deceased belonged to, the same set of laws have to be followed as far as registering a death is concerned. But once the paperwork has been done the family or community is free to conduct the funeral according to whatever religious or non-religious rites they wish, provided that these don't constitute a public nuisance of any kind.

In many parts of Britain every religious group has its own leaders who can be called in to arrange the funeral according to the requirements of the religion. In places where there is a high concentration of any particular religious group there may even be specially designated burial grounds – for example, Jews and Muslims have their own burial grounds in some cities.

Some of the more prominent groups who will want their own funeral arrangements are:

- Humanists

- Quakers

- Jews

- Muslims

- Buddhists

- Sikhs

- Hindus

- Confucians.

Understanding religious customs

Many of these religious groups don't like anyone other than the family to handle the body after death. For many, the body must be laid out and prepared for the funeral in a particular way.

Whatever the requirements, sensitivity can make things easier all round. Anyone who finds themselves having care of a dying member of any religion they don't understand should try to find someone who does understand to advise them on what should and should not be done.

Finding religious leaders

There are some parts of the country where only a few people from any one religion live and they don't have a religious leader among them. In that case a hospital or hospice social worker, a funeral director or crematorium or cemetery manager should normally be able to find out where the nearest leader of that religion lives and ask for them to come and arrange the funeral.

DISCOVERING ALTERNATIVES

It was mentioned in the last chapter that there are no laws about how a funeral has to be conducted, or that it has to have a religious component. The next of kin can conduct the funeral ceremony themselves if they want to, or ask anyone they consider appropriate to do the job for them. Any kind of readings or music can be used, or none at all.

The British Humanist Association and the Natural Death Centre both publish a lot of useful information about arranging non-religious funeral ceremonies. This kind of ceremony can be combined with a traditional type of burial or cremation managed by a funeral director, or it can be incorporated into one of many kinds of alternative funeral.

HAVING AN INDEPENDENT FUNERAL

Just as there is no law about how a funeral ceremony is organised, there is no law about how a body should be disposed of. A growing number of people prefer to save money and make the funerals of their friends and family more individual by doing as much as possible of the work themselves.

Some people like to call this a 'DIY funeral', others think that the term is misleading because there are several stages where professional help has to be employed. The term 'assisted' or 'independent' funeral has more meaning in a situation where the family would like to make their own arrangements within the framework of assistance provided by the hospitals, crematoria and cemetery authorities.

The next of kin are free to buy a coffin, lay out the body themselves, make the necessary arrangements at the crematorium or cemetery, arrive with the body in the coffin in their own vehicle, with their own pall bearers, and conduct their own ceremony.

It isn't always easy to buy a coffin but a few funeral directors do sell them to individuals and there are one or two firms that will deliver them, mail order. And, of course, any handy carpenter can make one.

It's also possible to arrange with a funeral director to use his services to transport the body, either from hospital or hospice to the family home, for laying out, or later to the crematorium or cemetery where the body can wait in the Chapel of Rest until the funeral takes place.

Advantages of independent arrangements

The advantages of these private arrangements are:

- a cheaper funeral

- the family is in control of the whole process

- the funeral can be better designed to suit the tastes and wishes of the family (and the deceased)

- some families may prefer that the deceased is not handled by strangers.

Disadvantages of independent arrangements

The disadvantages are:

- the next of kin has to do more form filling for the crematorium or cemetery (this is one of the professional duties undertaken by a funeral director)

- there may be problems buying a coffin at short notice

- some people may find the tasks connected with laying out a body difficult to cope with

- some families may be too stressed to handle all the additional work.

Laying out a body

There are those who feel that the attention of laying out a body is a final act of love they can perform for someone who has been close to them in life. They don't like the thought of strangers performing the intimate tasks that are necessary.

But the job shouldn't be undertaken without an understanding of what has to be done and a strongish stomach.

Crematoria have to insist that the body arrives 'in a sanitary condition', which means that all openings of the body need to be plugged because after death, when there is no more muscle control, the contents of the body will seep out.

The limbs have to be straightened and the eyes need to be closed to prevent a staring appearance. And unless the jaw is held shut in some way it will sag open. Common ways of closing the jaw are by a small bandage or by stitching the lower gums to the upper.

The body needs to be thoroughly washed and dressed either in a shroud or in the deceased's own clothes. A shroud is easier because once rigor mortis has set in it can be difficult to get limbs into sleeves and trousers. Finally the hair has to be arranged and sometimes the face made up – more usually in women to make them look as they used to when they were alive.

A funeral director is used to doing all these things and thinks nothing of it. If you think you would find them difficult but still want to arrange the funeral by yourselves, you may find that a district nurse or someone at the hospital or hospice will be able to help you. And if you do decide to do it yourself, the *Natural Death Handbook* from the Natural Death Centre gives detailed instructions on how to go about the job.

Applying for cremation

Some crematoria are owned by local authorities, some are owned by private companies. The forms that must be filled in by the next of kin to book a cremation are very simple. The following information is normally required, though every crematorium has its own individual variation of application form (Figure 6):

- full name and address of applicant

- full name and address of deceased

APPLICATION FOR CREMATION

WITH DECLARATION

Pursuant to the Regulations made by the Secretary of State for the Home Department,
dated 28 October 1930, 26 September 1952, and 15 May 1965

I *(full name of applicant)*, ... RAM SINGH ....

(Address) ..... 5, WHITE ROAD, ANYHAM ....

(Occupation or description) ... BUSINESS MAN ....

apply to the Anyham Crematorium Committee to undertake the cremation of the remains of

(Name of deceased) JASWANT KAUR SINGH ....

(Address) ... 5, WHITE ROAD, ANYHAM ....

(Occupation) HOUSEWIFE ....

(Age) 30 *(Sex)* F *(whether married, widow, widower or unmarried)* MARRIED ....

at the Anyham Crematorium   *(divorced)* ....

Each question must be answered

The true answers to the questions set out below are as follows:—

1.	Are you an executor or the nearest surviving relative of the deceased? *(If so,* **state which** *and define relationship, if any).*	YES – HUSBAND
2.	If not, state *(a)* Your relationship to the deceased. *(b)* The reason why the application is made by you and not by an executor or any nearer relative.	*(a)* — *(b)* —
3.	Have the near relatives of the deceased been informed of the proposed cremation?	YES
4.	Has any near relative of the deceased expressed any objection to the proposed cremation? If so, on what ground?	NO
5.	What was the date and hour of the death of the deceased?	7.30 PM 19 MARCH 199X
6.	What was the place where the deceased died? (Give address and say whether own residence, lodgings, hotel, hospital, nursing home, etc.)	ANYHAM GENERAL HOSPITAL
7.	Do you know or have you any reason to suspect that the death of the deceased was due, directly or indirectly to *(a)* violence; *(b)* poison; *(c)* privation or neglect?	a NO b NO c NO
8.	Do you know any reason whatever for supposing that an examination of the remains of the deceased may be desirable?	NO
9.	Give name and address of the ordinary medical attendant of the deceased.	DR GUDRUN KAUR
10.	Give names and addresses of the medical practitioners who attended deceased during his or her last illness.	DR JOHN SMITH DR ANN JONES

The following supplementary questions to Form 'B' have been approved by the Home Office.

(i)   Has the deceased been fitted with (a) a cardiac pacemaker? NO   *

(b) a radio-active or other implant? NO   *

(ii)   If the answer to (a) or (b) above is in the affirmative:
Has this been removed? .... *Answer separately

NOTE: CREMATION MAY BE REFUSED IF A PACEMAKER IS NOT REMOVED.

I DECLARE that to the best of my knowledge and belief the information given in this application correct and no material particular has been omitted.

(Signature) ..... Ram Singh ....

Date ..... 21 MARCH 199X ....

Fig. 6. Application for cremation.

- date, time and place of death

- relationship of applicant to deceased

- details of doctor who attended the deceased

- details of service to be conducted

- details of person to conduct service

- details of hymns or other music required

- whether bearers or a wheeled bier are required

- details of person who has prepared the body

- what is to be done with the cremated remains (Figure 7).

In some circumstances, you will also need a second medical certificate, signed by a doctor who is not a member of the same practice as the doctor who signed the original Certificate of Cause of Death. This can be arranged by your GP, by the hospital or hospice where the death took place, or by the crematorium.

The following regulations will have to be observed:

- All statutory forms must be received at the crematorium one working day before the cremation.

- All payments due must be made one working day before the cremation.

- The body must be hygienically prepared.

- The applicant must provide sufficient people to carry the coffin from the hearse or car to the wheeled bier provided by the crematorium.

- The coffin must bear the name of the deceased.

- The coffin must be within a specified size (to fit into the cremator).

AUTHORITY FOR DISPOSAL OF CREMATED REMAINS

I, being Applicant in Form 'A' overleaf for the cremation of the late...... JASWANT KAUR SINGH

......I, RAM SINGH............................ HEREBY AUTHORISE the cremated remains to be

(a) Rested at the discretion of the Crematorium Authority

(b) Disposal in a manner similar to that of ....

Cremated..

(c) Placed in Niche in Columbarium.

(d) Removed from the Crematorium by representative.

(e) If no decision has been reached, left in temporary deposit.

If an appointment is desired to witness the strewing or burial please indicate by a tick in this box ☐

Strike out alternatives not required

.... Ram Singh ....
Signature of Applicant for Cremation.

Address...5 WHITE ROAD ....

...... ANYHAM .... *Post Code* ....

Date .... 21 MARCH 199X

NOTE—All cremated remains left for disposal at the Crematorium are retained for one week to allow relatives time to alter their decision if they so wish. Where they are being held on Temporary Deposit a fee for their further retention will be payable after two months. The Committee reserves the right to dispose of them at its discretion after six months if such fees have not been paid.

Fig. 7. Authority for disposal of cremated remains.

- The coffin must be plain wood, not painted or varnished. The only metal used must be highly ferrous and then only if necessary – wooden plugs are preferred.

- No plastic, metal, rubber, pitch, sawdust or cotton wool may be used for decorating or lining the coffin.

- The body should be dressed only in natural materials.

The list looks daunting but the crematorium authorities are there to help and will make things as easy as possible.

Applying for burial

Cemeteries can be owned by local authorities or by the relevant religious authorities if they are attached to a place of religious worship. Many cemeteries are now full and can't be used for further burials. Information about local authority cemeteries can be obtained by telephoning the parks departments of your local authority, information about religious cemeteries from the relevant minister of religion.

The details needed to arrange a burial are similar to that for a cremation. The regulations on the construction of a coffin are not so strict and a few cemeteries will accept bodies for burial without coffins, in body bags or shrouds.

In most cemeteries the plot of land for a burial has to be bought if the family want exclusive right to it, and the rights purchased are usually limited to a period of up to 100 years. This time limit is because, eventually, the coffin and the body will rot away and disappear, the family will often lose interest in the grave, and the land will need to be reused.

Most cemeteries offer the option of burial in a 'common plot' which is cheaper than buying an individual plot. In that case a memorial stone won't be permitted, though there should be a place for a plaque. Once a family have bought a grave plot and put up a memorial they are responsible for its upkeep, though the owning authority is responsible for maintaining the general environment. It's likely that there will be strict rules about the type and size of memorial or headstone that can be erected.

Plots can also be bought for the burial of cremated remains. These are cheaper than graves because they are smaller. The burial of these remains is a different matter from the scattering of the ashes, which is usually free of charge.

There is usually also an additional charge for grave digging, which the authorities require should be done by their own employees for health and safety reasons. It's sometimes permitted for the mourners to fill in the grave themselves after the funeral.

BURYING IN OTHER PLACES

A 'back garden' burial

Just as there are no laws governing the way a funeral is conducted, there is no law that says a body must be buried in a recognised cemetery. You don't even need planning permission for a burial on private land, though there are environmental health regulations that have to be satisfied, related to the distance that the grave is to be from houses. Your local authority will give you information about this.

A burial of this kind is a nice idea if there is plenty of land available, but it could cause problems in a small garden, specially if the family later want to move house.

A woodland burial

A comparatively recent idea is to manage what are commonly called 'woodland burial' sites. These are ecologically friendly burial grounds where the only memorial for every grave is a tree planted over the grave, to feed on the decaying body. Some grounds also provide a memorial wall where the people buried there are remembered by a small plaque.

The environment is kept like a nature reserve, as natural as possible with the idea that people can walk around and enjoy the woodland.

More and more of this kind of burial ground are being brought into use. Some are owned by local authorities, some by private concerns. An up to date list of where they are can be obtained from the Natural Death Centre, or from Heaven on Earth, which calls itself the first 'Design your Life and Death' shop (see Useful Addresses).

KNOWING YOUR RIGHTS

The Institute of Burial and Cremation Administration (IBCA), worried about the poor service a lot of people were getting, recently produced a Charter for the Bereaved, specially designed to improve funerals.

The Charter aims to make people less frightened of dealing with death and more aware of the choices they have when planning funerals. It sets out 33 basic rights, including your right to a dignified and orderly funeral, and to full knowledge about all the alternatives available.

One of the most complete and all-embracing funeral services in the country is provided by Carlisle City Council. Through what it calls its 'Bereavement Services' it provides the whole range of directed funerals with cremations, cemetery or woodland burial. It also provides help and advice for families who want to arrange funerals themselves, which it calls independent cremations and burials. Even if you don't live anywhere near Carlisle it is worth sending for their information pack if only to find out what you should have the right to expect from your own authorities.

BURYING AT SEA

Sea burials are something of a tradition in Britain for those whose lives have been in some way connected with the sea, and some people request this kind of disposal in their will. This can make the funeral both difficult and expensive for the next of kin. Although in theory it's perfectly possible to bury at sea the authorities don't encourage this because of the problems that can be caused. For example:

- The body might be moved around by tides and currents and be washed up on the shore.

- The body might be brought up in the nets of a trawler.

- Bodies of people who have suffered from certain types of infection may contaminate the environment and the food chain.

- The attending mourners may suffer from seasickness which could make the funeral a more unpleasant experience than it need be.

However, because it's recognised that some people may feel strongly about the matter, sea burials are allowed providing certain regulations are obeyed.

Observing the regulations
These regulations are laid down in the Food and Environment Protection Act 1985 and administered by the Ministry of Agriculture, Fisheries and Food in England and Wales, and the Agriculture and Fisheries Department of The Scottish Office in Scotland. They are

designed to make sure the body sinks to the bottom of the sea and stays there, and decomposes as quickly as possible.

They also govern where the burial can take place. It's not possible to hire a boat and just go out and bury a body anywhere at sea. There are approved burial sites, one off Newhaven and one off the western end of the Isle of Wight. For Scotland, there is one approximately 210 nautical miles west of Oban and 15 miles west of John O'Groats, north of Dunnet Head. Other sites may be given special approval.

Obtaining a sea burial licence

An application has to be made by telephoning the District Inspector responsible for the burial site (details from the relevant Ministry) who will give information about the regulations and will issue a certificate in the form of a letter.

The authorities don't make any of the arrangements. It's up to the next of kin to find a funeral director who is willing to do this kind of funeral, such as the Britannia Shipping Company, or to make their own arrangements for transport of the coffin, a suitable boat with the necessary lifting gear, and any ceremony they want.

Scattering of ashes at sea

Much easier than arranging a burial at sea is the disposal of cremated remains at sea. If the ashes are to be thrown into the sea in some kind of container a licence is still needed because the authorities want to make sure that the container will sink, but the list of regulations is not so long.

A far more commonly used alternative is simply to scatter the loose ashes on the water, with a suitable ceremony, for which no licence or special arrangements are required.

CHECKLIST

1. A lot of people in Britain don't want a traditional Christian-based funeral.

2. Everyone is entitled to a funeral conducted by a leader of their own religion, or to a non-religious funeral.

3. A family is entitled to do all the work of conducting a funeral themselves, including laying out the body.

4. A burial doesn't necessarily have to be in a recognised cemetery.

5. Burials at sea are possible but strictly controlled.

CASE STUDIES

Jane has a simple Humanist ceremony

Before Jane died she discussed her funeral wishes with Ralph. She wanted a cremation, arranged by a funeral director, to spare her family the extra work. As she didn't believe in God, she contacted the British Humanist Association to talk over and plan a simple ceremony with a Humanist officiant. When the time comes, the funeral director collects her body from the hospice and prepares it for the cremation in a plain style of coffin. The Humanist officiant comes to lead the ceremony in the crematorium chapel, at which Ralph and the three children all give readings that Jane chose. After the ceremony the mourners are all invited back to the family house for a buffet lunch where Jane is the main topic of conversation.

A few days after the cremation the family collect the ashes and together they scatter them in the woodland where they used to take family walks.

Jaswant's family follow their religion

Jaswant's body is moved from the mortuary to an undertaker's parlour where, on the morning of the funeral, her female relatives go to wash the body, and dress it in a new red dress. Then, with the help of the undertaker, they put the body in the coffin. The coffin goes first to Ram's house, which is by then full of female mourners from the surrounding Sikh community who have come to pay their respects. There the Granthi (priest) reads from the Guru Granth Sahib (the holy book).

A short time before the cremation has been booked the body is taken to the nearby Sikh temple where the male mourners are waiting and the Granthi says a few short prayers. Then two coaches arrive so that everyone can follow the hearse and the family cars to the crematorium. The crematorium chapel is too small for everyone, but they all gather outside and listen as the Granthi says more prayers. Then the Granthi and the close family members go into the cremating area and watch while the coffin is put into the cremator. As soon as this happens the Granthi recites a prayer known as the Kirtan Soila. It's expected that everyone will have a good cry.

The family and some of their close friends then go back to the Sikh temple where they eat a special dish of parshad (sweet semolina and butter) that the Granthi has prepared and read verses from the Alanaian, a special section of the holy book. Then the women and children go to Ram's home and in the temple Ram and his male relatives prepare a meal for all the remaining guests, sending portions home for the women and children. Then starts the Akhand Path, a marathon 48 hour reading of holy verses in Ram's home. When this is over, Ram and his family collect Jaswant's ashes from the crematorium and, with further prayers, scatter them in the fresh running water of a nearby river.

DISCUSSION POINTS

1. Do you have a clear idea of what is involved in arranging a funeral?

2. How would you feel about laying out a body yourself?

3. Do you know where to find help in organising an independent funeral?

6
Paying the Bills

A CONTINUING FINANCIAL LIFE

Some people manage to live and die free of the burdens associated with money, but in the normal run of things most people have a complicated financial life. When a person dies that financial life doesn't automatically come to an end. It continues for some time with a momentum of its own. There are still bills to be paid for the household expenses, for the funeral, for loan repayments and other standing orders. The next of kin or executor has to deal with all this.

INFORMING BANKS AND BUILDING SOCIETIES

The first thing that needs to be done on behalf of the deceased is to inform the bank and or building society about the death. They will want to know the date of the death and to receive as soon as possible a copy of the Death Certificate issued by the Registrar's office, or a Coroner's Interim Certificate.

Dealing with joint accounts
If the deceased held joint accounts with another person, the other person can continue to use the account and everything in it automatically belongs to that other person.

If there was more than one other person involved, the remaining people share the account assets equally. As soon as they see the copy of the Death Certificate the bank will transfer the account into the name(s) of the surviving signatory(ies).

This also applies to business accounts unless the constitution of the business states otherwise.

Dealing with sole accounts in the name of the deceased
If the accounts were in the name of the deceased only, these will be

frozen until grant of probate or confirmation is obtained (see next chapter). Any cheques written before the death will be honoured – provided there is enough money in the account.

The only things for which money will be released prior to probate are:

- payment of the funeral account

- probate fees

- payments to the Inland Revenue on which probate or confirmation is dependent.

These payments are entirely at the discretion of individual banks and building societies – there is no legal requirement for them to be allowed. Some banks prefer to arrange a bridging loan for these rather than pay out of the 'frozen' account.

Banks may also take money due for settlement of a loan or credit card account before the grant of probate. They will certainly always hold back such money before paying over the balance to an executor.

PAYING FOR THE FUNERAL

Spending money on a funeral

Some people think that cutting costs on a funeral shows disrespect for the dead person. They believe that an expensive funeral gives a really good send off. Others believe that it's only sensible to spend as little as possible on a funeral because no amount of money will help the dead and it's better saved for the living. And some people have no choice but to spend as little as possible.

Who pays for a funeral?

The person who pays is normally the deceased. It's a legal requirement, written automatically into a person's will, that payment for the funeral comes ahead of payment of any other creditors. This payment is automatically deducted from the funds of the deceased before calculations are made for other bequests.

There are, of course, many cases where other members of the family will pay for a funeral, particularly in the case of a young person, or a spouse without money of their own. If a funeral director is handling the funeral they will normally ask at the time it is being arranged who is to receive the account.

Some funeral directors will insist on payment in advance, but most will present a bill shortly after the funeral and expect it to be settled without too much delay because they will already have paid out money for the coffin, the vehicles, the crematorium or cemetery and the relevant ministers.

In the case of funerals arranged without a funeral director, the person doing the arranging will have to make all these payments as the arrangements are made, so will need to make sure that the money is to hand.

Understanding the cost

Many families worry in advance about the cost of funerals. Some never give it a thought until the time comes and get a nasty shock. In times past people used to save up for their funerals even if they had nothing else to their name. It was a matter of pride to be able to afford a decent burial and this attitude still prevails in some communities.

People like to complain that funeral directors make a lot of money out of death. But in general, if all the outlay and capital investment is added up, the profit margin generally seems quite fair in view of the amount of work done.

Every funeral director will give the family a wide choice of how much they can spend. There will be choices about:

- the type and style of coffin

- the provision of mourners' cars

- the provision of pall bearers

- arranging the refreshments afterwards

- providing permanent memorials

- keeping lists of who sends flowers and/or donations to charity

- bereavement counselling services.

In addition, the further the body has to be transported the more the funeral will cost, so a funeral going straight to the crematorium will be much cheaper than one that includes a stop-off for a church service as well. Taking a body to a different part of the country for burial will be very expensive, though sometimes this is unavoidable.

All the charges involved should be made clear beforehand by the funeral director. Problems sometimes occur because of the shock factor – people suffering immediately after a bereavement don't always take in everything that is said to them. So, once again, it's a good idea to take a friend or relative to help make the funeral arrangements.

Calculating the cost using a funeral director

At the present time (1996) the basic plan provided through Chosen Heritage, the pre-paid funeral system recommended by Age Concern, costs £695. This covers:

* guidance on the certification and registration of death

* removal of the body to the funeral director's premises (within UK)

* laying out the body (but not viewing)

* basic coffin

* provision of hearse to meet the family at the crematorium or cemetery (does not include processions, or church service)

* staff for the funeral service.

This plan does not include crematorium or cemetery fees, minister's or doctor's fees, which would come to around a further £400.

The most basic plan offered by the Funeral Centre, a large organisation in Catford, East London, costs £495, again plus the additional payments mentioned above.

Green Undertakings say they can arrange a 'good' funeral for around £350, plus the additional payments.

This means that, using a funeral director, the very cheapest price will come to a total of just under £800. So it should be possible to arrange a plain but adequate funeral through a funeral director for between £800 and £1500. It is, of course, possible to spend a great deal more.

Calculating the cost of an independent funeral

The costs of an independent funeral can vary just as much as the cost of using a funeral director, but it is possible to get a cheaper package this way.

For example, prices quoted by Carlisle City Council Bereavement Services (1996) are as follows:

- Cremation fees – £192, less for children (includes doctor's certificate).

- Burial fees – £170 for a resident, £185 for a non-resident, less for children.

- Woodland grave – £91.50.

- Chapel of Rest for 24 hours – £8.25.

Carlisle offer a complete independent 'environmental cremation' service, using a bio-degradable coffin and accepting that cremation may not take place up to 24 hours after the service, for £395. Their independent burial cost, using a recycled grave and bio-degradable coffin, is £343. These costs include a minister or officiant and a funeral director's hearse to transport the coffin.

Budgeting for yourself
If you live in a place where a package such as this isn't available, the following must be budgeted for on top of crematorium or cemetery costs:

A coffin
You may be able to buy a coffin from a local funeral director but they aren't all helpful about this. There are some mail-order options:

- Green Undertakings can supply oak-veneered chipboard from £78, pine from £220, recycled woods from £165, wicker from £250, cardboard from £55.

- Compakta Limited supply a cardboard coffin at £39.95 plus £12.93 delivery.

- Carlisle City Bereavement Services supply bio-degradable coffins at £57 and £108, oak-veneered chipboard at £123.

- Solid wood coffins are rarely used nowadays and cost in the region of £500 or more.

A body bag
In some places this is an acceptable alternative to a coffin. Green Undertakings supply a bio-degradable bag from £12, a heavy-duty bag from £48. Carlisle supply a bag with carrying ropes and board for £120.

Transport
Funeral directors in Carlisle quoted between £56 and £100 for a hearse to pick up a coffin, collect a body from the mortuary and transport both to the crematorium. You don't have to have a hearse to do this, a van or estate car large enough to take a coffin will do.

Minister's or officiant's fees
If you don't want to conduct the ceremony yourselves, these will be normally around £60 plus travelling expenses.

A memorial
This can vary from a few pounds for a plaque to hundreds for a gravestone. In some places a 'home made' one would be allowed, but some cemeteries and crematoria are very fussy.

All these prices were correct in 1996.

Being unable to pay
There are cases when somebody dies with no next of kin to see to a burial. This can happen in old people's homes, or in shelters for vagrants. In cases where the deceased is obviously not in a position to pay it is the responsibility of the relevant local authority to arrange and pay for a funeral.

There are also cases, probably not so rare, when a family simply doesn't have the money to pay for a funeral. This could be a family living on Social Security but could also simply be a family with no resources. In a situation like this the local authority can be asked to pay for the funeral.

However, it is important to understand that the local authority must be approached before the funeral is arranged, because they have special contracts with certain funeral directors. It's no good going along to them with the account after the funeral has taken place because they can't help then.

APPLYING FOR GRANTS AND PENSIONS

Applying for state benefits

When a death is registered the Registrar will provide a booklet giving information about state benefits that may be available and a form to send to the Social Security office.

According to the circumstances you have been left in these might include:

- a widow's payment (tax free lump sum)

- a widow's pension (for widows over 45)

- a widowed mother's allowance

- maternity benefit

- additional retirement pension

- incapacity benefits (if your spouse died as a result of industrial injury or disablement)

- one parent benefit

- guardian's allowance (if you are bringing up an orphaned child)

- income support

- family credit

- housing benefit

- council tax benefit.

Receiving other pensions

There is a wide range of other private pension, insurance and annuity schemes that may entitle a widow or widower to lump sum payments or regular income.

The proceeds of any life insurance policy, which should be wound up by the executor, become part of the estate of the deceased, unless any particular person was named as beneficiary or the policy is tied in with the mortgage on a house. This means that a widow or widower doesn't automatically get the whole of the proceeds of a policy: it may have to be divided amongst other people named in the will.

Every pension scheme and insurance policy may be different, with different conditions, and it is up to the executor to check all this out.

DOING THE HOUSEKEEPING

In the weeks immediately after a death or a funeral the people left behind have to continue with their lives. This means eating, travelling, paying the gas and electricity bills and generally keeping everything going.

If the deceased had all his or her money in a sole account which is frozen at death, the remaining partner and/or dependent children can find themselves in difficulties. Some will readily be able to go to other relatives for help, others may not like to ask.

If there is money in the bank, the bank will often be sympathetic and make a small loan to tide over the dependants until the money becomes theirs. If the money is in a post office account this can be transferred very quickly because the same rules about waiting for a Grant of Probate don't apply, all that is needed is a copy of the Death Certificate.

If there is no money or insurance policy and income suddenly stops because of the death of the breadwinner, the dependants must apply to the nearest Social Security office for help.

CHECKLIST

1. Banks and/or building societies where the deceased held accounts must be informed about the death.

2. Joint account holders will be able to continue to use the account.

3. Accounts only in the name of the deceased will be frozen.

4. The funeral is paid for out of the money left by the deceased.

5. A funeral can be paid for by the local authority.

6. State benefits may be available for the next of kin.

CASE STUDIES

Ralph loses Jane's pension

Ralph and Jane have already set aside money to pay for both their funerals so the final bill of £1,850 doesn't come as a shock. As all their other assets – car, house, bank and savings accounts – are in joint names, it is automatically all transferred to Ralph's name as soon as he sends the copies of the Death Certificate to the right places. As soon as they hear from the Registrar, the local authority pensions department stop Jane's pension which Ralph will now have to manage without. As he has an adequate pension of his own he isn't entitled to any further grants or benefits.

Isabel has trouble paying the bills

Isabel has never had any money or a bank account of her own. Alistair always paid all the bills and gave her the housekeeping money in cash. Now, apart from a few pounds she has saved in an old tea-caddy, she has nothing to either buy food or pay the bills for the funeral and the running of the farm. She goes to Alistair's bank with Ian and talks to the manager, who is prepared to release money to pay the funeral account of £2,000 and to make a loan for enough to pay the farm and household expenses for three months. Ian has to sign that he is responsible for this loan because the farm runs on an overdraft system and may eventually have to be sold to clear its debt.

Ram borrows from the bank

Although Ram has no problem with getting money out of the bank, the funeral is very expensive for him. As well as paying the undertaker and the crematorium, he has to provide food and transport for over a hundred people and new clothes for Jaswant to be laid out in. There are also items such as a new set of clothes, linen, food, and a set of plates, cups and bowls which are given to the Granthi for Jaswant to use in the afterlife. Although Ram's family's shop is prosperous they haven't got all that much ready cash, but Ram is able to borrow what is necessary from the bank, guaranteed by his father. The Registrar has told Ram that he will be entitled to a single parent's allowance from the date of Jaswant's death, but he hasn't applied for it yet.

DISCUSSION POINTS

1. Do you understand the responsibilities of banks and building societies after the death of a customer?

2. How would you manage financially if your partner died?

3. How could the cost of a funeral be cut down if there wasn't enough money to pay for it?

7
Acting as Executor

CARRYING OUT LEGAL DUTIES

What being an executor means

The legal duties of an executor are basically to deal with the estate of the dead person.

In this case, 'estate' means everything that has been left, minus outstanding debts. So, in effect, the executor has to sort out all the financial affairs of the dead person, make sure all debts are paid and the money and property that remains is shared out according to the will, if there is one, or according to inheritance law if there is no will.

In practice, if the executor is also a member of the family or a close friend, they may also play a large part in organising the funeral. A solicitor would only do this if specifically instructed by the deceased or the family.

Anyone can be an executor as long as they can fill in forms efficiently. It does take up a bit of time and means quite a lot of running around and telephoning to various offices. Because of this, sometimes a person will appoint two people to be co-executors. It is normal, when making a will, to ask the chosen person or people first if they will do the job and to leave some small sum of money in token of the amount of work that will be involved.

A person appointed as an executor is free to refuse to undertake the responsibility when the time comes, even if they have previously agreed. In that case someone else in the family can take on the job, or a solicitor can be appointed.

Using a solicitor

Many people name a solicitor as executor in their will. Solicitors will certainly be less likely to make legal mistakes and should be able to sort everything efficiently and as quickly as possible (though some solicitors have been known to drag their feet in these matters).

The executor(s) have the option of employing a solicitor rather than doing the job themselves. The big advantage of this is that the executor is legally responsible if any mistakes are made and this could be expensive.

The solicitor, whether acting as executor or employed by the executor, will of course, need to be paid. Charges vary, but will take upwards of £500 from even a modest estate.

NOTIFYING CREDITORS

It's the responsibility of the next of kin or the executor to tell all the creditors of the deceased about the death and ask them to make a claim – in other words ask them to send in their bills.

Who is a creditor?
Any one to whom the deceased owes money at the time of death. Once probate has been obtained the executor must pay all creditors before any bequests made in the will can be paid. Creditors might be:

- banks, building societies or credit companies who have made loans (unless the loans are covered by insurance schemes)

- shops or mail order companies

- courts of law

- people on whose behalf a court order has been made (ex-spouses, children of previous marriages)

- business suppliers.

In addition, any person who was being supported financially by the deceased can make a claim.

Finding all the creditors
Most of the creditors can be discovered by going through the papers and accounts kept by the deceased but the executors should also put an advertisement in the local paper, and possibly also the *London Gazette*, just to make sure everyone who has a claim knows about the death.

Creditors must make their claims within six months. After that the money will be distributed to the beneficiaries and it will be too late.

CLAIMING LIFE INSURANCE

Any life assurance companies must be told about the death as soon as possible and it's the job of the executor or whoever is dealing with the estate to do this. The life insurance company will require a copy of the Death Certificate, but they will only make further enquiries before paying out if there is any kind of criminal investigation going on, or if the deceased committed suicide within a minimum period stated on the policy (usually within a year of taking out the policy).

APPLYING FOR PROBATE – ENGLAND AND WALES

What is probate?

To be strictly correct, we should be talking about a Grant of Representation, or Letters of Administration, issued by the Probate Registry in England and Wales.

This isn't the sort of grant that means money will be given out, it is a formal document that gives the person(s) applying the power to administer the estate of the deceased. This is because organisations such as banks or companies holding the money of the deceased need proof of whom they should pay it to.

Managing without a grant of probate

There are circumstances in which a grant isn't necessary, all that is needed is a copy of the Death Certificate. These are:

- when property is held in joint names

- when bank or building society accounts are held in joint names

- when money is held in a post office account

- when money held in a bank or building society is what is called a 'small estate' – less than £5000.

However, although the law allows banks and building societies to release funds of under £5000 without probate, it doesn't say they have to and it is best to find out the situation from every company individually.

Who can apply for the grant of probate?

The law lays down a strict order of precedence as to who may apply for the grant, starting with the named executor and going through to any creditor, if nobody else is interested in doing it. This precedence is useful because it prevents any sort of quarrels arising over the matter and it means that creditors can take independent steps to get their money back if necessary.

More than one person, up to a maximum of four, can apply for the grant together.

Making the application
There are several stages to applying without using a solicitor:

1. Finding out whether there is a will or not.

2. Listing the assets and debts of the estate.

3. Deciding where you want to be interviewed by the probate officer.

4. Sending for the application forms.

5. Completing the forms.

6. Sending the forms back to the Registry.

7. Making an appointment and attending the interview.

8. Paying fees and taxes.

There will also be forms to complete for the Capital Taxes Office of the Inland Revenue.

If it turns out that there is more than one will in existence, the latest is the legal one. However, a will doesn't have to be dated to be legal and sometimes other evidence has to be taken to the probate office to prove which is the latest will.

The only exception to this is when someone has married after making their last will, in which case the will is invalid and the intestacy laws must apply (except if the will has been changed shortly before marriage and states that this is because of the intention to marry).

The nearest convenient local probate office can be found from the telephone directory. The executor should telephone the office to ask for a set of forms to be sent.

All the completed forms, together with the Death Certificate (copy from the Registrar's office) and the original of the will (if any), should be sent back to the probate office. Remember to keep a copy of the will because the original doesn't get returned, it goes to the Public Records Office.

If there are no queries, the probate office will give an appointment for an interview within ten working days of receiving the forms. If there are any problems they will contact the applicant to clear these up within the ten days. The interview is to confirm the details in the forms and to swear an oath to support the information given.

Paying the probate fees

If there is no inheritance tax owing the only thing remaining to be done is to pay the probate registry fees. There are two types of fee:

1. A court fee, paid on estates larger than £10,000 by either solicitors or personal applicants

2. A personal application fee paid by personal applicants only.

Both sets of fees are banded according to the size of the estate and can't be fixed until the interview, but a guide is sent out with the forms so that people have some idea of how much they will have to pay. The sum varies from £1 for an estate of £500 to a total of £500 for an estate of £200,000.

Waiting for the grant

Even if there is no tax to pay, the applicant won't receive the grant of probate right away because everything has to be sent to the District Registry to be checked and signed. This will take another two weeks. Then the applicant is sent a bound copy of the grant with a copy of the will attached to it, and as many copies of the grant as were asked for at the time of the interview.

It can easily take up to two months for this process even if everything is straightforward. In complicated cases it can drag on for much longer. Until the grant of probate has been received there is no way the executor or any other applicant dealing with the estate can legally pay out or dispose of any of the estate to anyone, other than for funeral expenses.

These procedures are exactly the same if someone has died intestate – that is, without making a will. The only difference is that the applicant has to swear a slightly different form of oath, and the grant doesn't have a copy of a will attached to it.

APPLYING FOR CONFIRMATION – SCOTLAND

In Scotland the procedures are different and an executor has to apply for confirmation to the estate from the Commissary Office. In all parts of Scotland except Edinburgh the local Sheriff Clerk is also the Commissary Clerk and applicants for confirmation should go to the Sheriff Court nearest to the home of the deceased person.

Applying to be executor of an intestate estate

If a person dies without making a will, or without naming an executor, the nearest surviving relative needs to apply to the Sheriff Court to be appointed as executor dative. If there is any doubt as to who counts as the next surviving relative, the Sheriff Clerk will advise on this. A petition to act as executor is then publicly displayed by the Sheriff Clerk for nine days to allow for any objection.

Anyone, other than a surviving husband or wife inheriting the whole estate, who is acting as executor for an intestate estate, has to take out a 'bond of caution' (pronounced cay-shun). This bond, normally purchased from an insurance company but sometimes in the form of a guarantee from a private individual, insures the executor against any mistakes that might be made in the administration of the estate.

After confirmation has been obtained, the executor then has to distribute the estate according to the law – the Rights of Succession.

Administering a small estate

In Scotland a small estate is up to £17,000 and the Commissary or Sheriff Clerk will be able to help applicants to complete the paperwork for this, unless the estate involves what is known as 'heritable property' – houses or land. This is because of problems of valuation.

The executor's first duty is to make an inventory of the estate (a list of all available information about the estate's assets, including details of all insurance policies, and debts), in consultation with the Sheriff Clerk if help is needed. He or she should then attend at the Sheriff Clerk's office with the inventory, the death certificate and the will if there is one and complete Inland Revenue Form B3. It isn't necessary to make a prior appointment for this, but time can be saved by a telephone call when the Sheriff Clerk will also answer any preliminary questions that may have arisen.

If the will hasn't been witnessed it may be necessary for the executor to bring two witnesses who can identify the handwriting or signature of the deceased.

The executor will then have to swear an oath to support the information in the inventory, and will then have to leave the inventory and will with the Sheriff Clerk. Within a few days the Clerk will forward to the executor the confirmation, with the will attached, and the executor can proceed with the administration of the estate. The Clerk will also send a copy of the inventory to the Capital Taxes Office, even though no tax is due.

If it's impossible for the executor to attend the Sheriff Clerk's office in person the procedure can be completed by post, with the necessary oaths being administered by a Notary Public or JP. However, this may take longer.

Administering a large estate

In the case of an estate over £17,000, or an estate with heritable property, the Sheriff Clerk is still responsible for issuing the confirmation but cannot assist with the completion of the inventory because of possible complications. In these cases there is nothing to prevent an executor applying in person but because of difficulties in providing accurate valuations, and in disposing of heritable property, executors are advised to work through a solicitor.

Paying Commissary fees

In Scotland there is no fee on an estate of up to £5000. For an estate of between £5000 and £50,000 the fee is £70 and over £50,000 it is £100.

DISPUTING A GRANT OF PROBATE OR CONFIRMATION

It is possible to stop a grant of probate or confirmation being issued, or even to have it revoked after issue. For example, some long-lost member of a family might re-appear, or someone might find a will that they consider to be more recent than the one that has been proved. They can apply for a caveat to be put on the probate or confirmation until a court judgement has been made. This can lead to an expensive and long drawn out legal battle and it's advisable to consult a solicitor or the Citizens' Advice Bureau before taking action of this kind.

Any such dispute in England and Wales goes to the Chancery Division of the High Court, in Scotland to the Court of Session in Edinburgh, to be settled by a judge.

Remember that neither the probate officer at the Registry nor the Sheriff Clerk can give a legal opinion; he or she can only act on the documents as they are.

PAYING INHERITANCE TAXES

There are two types of estate for tax purposes. These are:

1. An 'excepted' estate where the total value of what has been left is less than £180,000 (unless the deceased gave away property within seven years of death, or lived outside the United Kingdom).

2. A 'non-excepted' estate, with a total value of more than £180,000 (including the value of gifts made in the last seven years).

The figure of £180,000 applied in 1996 but does change from time to time. It may sound like a lot of money but anyone owning even a modest family home in some parts of the country, plus a life insurance policy, will soon be over the limit.

Dealing with an 'excepted' estate

In England and Wales, at the same time as filling in the probate application form, the executor completes a form (IHT 205) for the Inland Revenue Capital Tax Office. In Scotland the form (B4) is part of the inventory form to be completed for the confirmation application.

In England and Wales the form then goes to the probate registry with the other documents, in Scotland the form and the inventory go to the Sheriff Clerk, and the forms are then sent on to the relevant Capital Tax Office.

In most excepted estates there is nothing more to be done as far as the Inland Revenue is concerned. However, you must keep the form because the Capital Tax Office do spot checks on a small proportion of cases every year and they have the right to ask you to fill in a full account within 35 days of the issue of the grant or confirmation.

Dealing with a 'non-excepted' estate

In England and Wales the applicant must complete form IHT 44 and also IHT 37 and IHT 40 if the deceased had an interest in any house or land, and/or in any stocks or shares. In Scotland the form to use is Form A3.

In England and Wales the probate officer will check these forms and then after the interview will send them on to the Capital Taxes Office for assessment. The tax office will then contact the applicant directly and the tax will have to be paid within six months. Only when the officer hears from the Tax Office that the tax has been paid can the grant of probate, or confirmation, be issued.

In Scotland the applicant must send the form straight to the Capital Taxes Office with the amount of tax that is owing on everything other than heritable property. The Capital Taxes Office returns the receipted form to the executor, who can then take or send them to the Sheriff Clerk for confirmation to be issued. The executor has six months to pay tax owing on heritable property.

When there is difficulty finding enough money to pay the taxes before the estate can be used, a bank loan can be arranged so that the tax can be settled, then the bank is paid as soon as the grant or confirmation is obtained. In other cases the solicitor or the executor would pay out of their own account, then claim back the amount owing, plus interest.

DISTRIBUTING THE ESTATE

Following the instructions in a will
Eventually the executor comes to the nicest part of the whole job, distributing the estate. This means following the instructions in the will to the letter about who is to have what, be it cash or assets.

However, the executor should either wait until six months after the death to do this, to allow creditors time to make their claims, or keep back sufficient money to pay any possible claims until after the six months has passed.

Making a distribution where there is no will
If the deceased was intestate, the law sets out an order of entitlement to the estate. This is known as the law of intestacy in England and Wales, and the right of succession in Scotland. The rules of entitlement are fairly complicated, depending on whether the deceased was married or not, had children or not, and the actual amount of money left, but the general principle is that the money passes down through the nearest living members of the family. Full information about this can be obtained from the Probate Registry or Commissary Office. If the deceased was intestate and had no living relatives, the entire estate becomes the property of the Crown.

Selling assets
There is one more hurdle to overcome, if there are assets such as a house or land, stocks and shares, or some other property such as antiques or pictures or vehicles to be sold so that the proceeds can

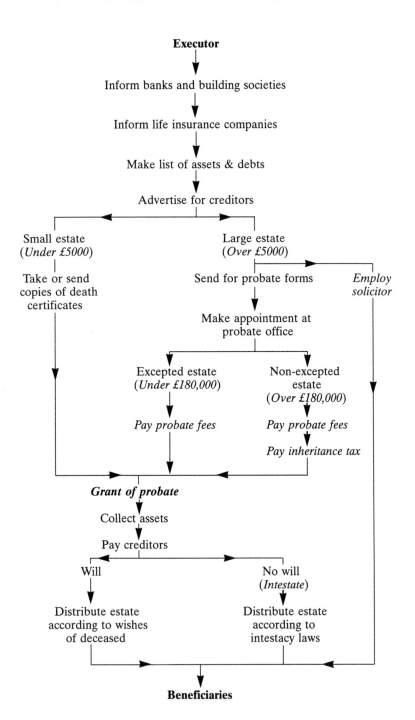

Fig. 8. Acting as executor – England and Wales.
(Procedures in N. Ireland are similar but have some differences.)

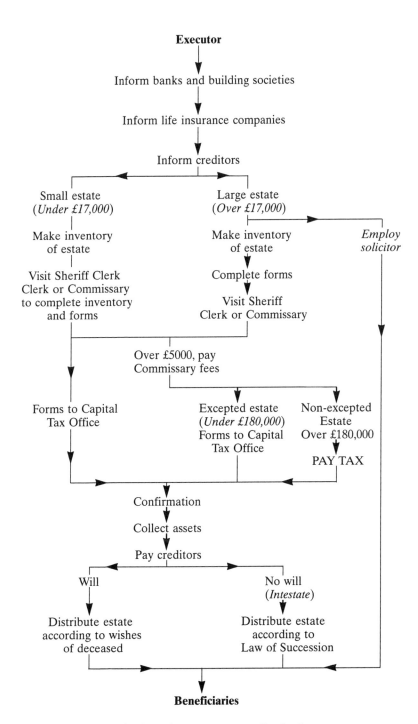

Fig. 9. Acting as executor – Scotland.

be distributed as cash.

The sale must take place as quickly as possible, and in any case should be within a year of the death, and for the best possible price at the time. As the money comes in, the executor may feel more comfortable opening a special bank account so that it can be accounted for more easily, especially if large sums are concerned, but there is no law that says this is necessary.

If a house or other special asset is taking a long time to sell, the beneficiaries (those inheriting the estate) may agree to a distribution of what is available by the end of the year, only receiving the proceeds of the sale when it finally becomes available.

If there isn't enough money in the estate to pay all the legacies, they should be reduced by equal proportions.

Missing beneficiaries

The only remaining complication is when one of the beneficiaries can't be found, even after official enquiries and advertising. In this case the share due to that person can be paid into the Chancery Division of the High Court to be held in case the person later turns up. Or the executor can buy an indemnity from an insurance company so that if necessary the insurance company will pay the missing beneficiary's share.

CHECKLIST

1. An executor's duties are to sort out the financial affairs of the deceased.

2. The executor or next of kin must apply for a grant of probate in England, Wales and Northern Ireland.

3. It will be necessary to apply for confirmation in Scotland.

4. It will be necessary to send information to the Inland Revenue.

5. The applicant who receives the grant or confirmation must distribute the estate according to the will.

6. If there is no will the estate must be distributed according to the law of intestacy in England and Wales or the right of succession in Scotland.

CASE STUDIES

Ralph needn't apply for probate

Because everything Jane owned was held jointly with Ralph, she effectively has no estate except for some costume jewellery and her clothes, which certainly don't amount to more than £5000. Therefore there is no need for a Grant of Probate and no tax is owing to the Capital Taxes Office.

Isabel must obtain confirmation

Alistair left no will so Isabel and Ian go to the Sheriff Officer and ask for Isabel to be appointed executor dative. Then, because the farm accounts seem very complicated and there is a bank overdraft to be dealt with, she and Ian take all Alistair's papers to a solicitor for advice. The title of the farm goes to Isabel, but because Ian isn't prepared to take on the responsibility of running it, they decide that Isabel should sell up and use the proceeds to pay off the bank overdraft and buy herself a small place to live. There won't be much left over from this so Ian must look for work and a place to live elsewhere.

Ram keeps Jaswant's dowry

Jaswant and Ram held everything in joint names so Jaswant's share of the bank account, the shop and their home all pass to Ram. She came to the marriage with an extensive dowry in terms of money, gold jewellery and household goods but, according to custom, all these now belong to Ram. His turn to pay out will come when his daughter marries and he has to provide her with a dowry.

DISCUSSION POINTS

1. Are you clear about the duties of an executor?

2. Do you understand the purpose of an application for probate or confirmation?

3. How does an executor find the creditors of the deceased?

4. Would you want to consider appointing a solicitor to act on your behalf as executor?

8
Disposing of Personal Effects

DEFINING 'PERSONAL EFFECTS'

Part of the executor's job is to estimate the value of all the possessions of the deceased, including the things defined by law as 'personal chattels', which we generally call 'personal effects'. These are:

- carriages, horses, stable furniture and effects

- motor cars and accessories

- garden effects

- domestic animals

- plate and plated articles

- linen, china and glass

- books, pictures, prints

- furniture

- jewellery

- articles of household or personal use or ornament

- musical and scientific instruments and apparatus

- wines, liquors and consumable stores.

These are sometimes more difficult to deal with than vast estates.

They are all supposed to be sold in such a way as to raise as much money as possible on behalf of the beneficiaries, or to settle outstanding debts. In reality these things will raise very little money compared with the trouble it will take to sell them.

Where grant of probate or confirmation is to be applied for, nothing should be given away or otherwise disposed of until after the grant has been obtained, even if individual items are specified in the will.

For most people, however, these personal bits and pieces are all that they leave and, with no property of value and therefore no probate involved, it falls on the next of kin to sort out and throw out or otherwise dispose of what is left.

CONSULTING THE FAMILY

Some people leave a letter or clear written instructions about who is to do what with their things, others don't even think about it.

In this situation, however much the executor or next of kin may feel themselves entitled to act independently, making decisions without consulting the rest of the family can lead to quarrels and resentment months, and even years, later.

It only takes a short time to make a few telephone calls, or write letters to other relatives, to say you are going to sort out the deceased's possessions and ask if that's all right with them and if there's anything they particularly want to keep. Whatever their reply, it puts you in the clear if there are any disputes later.

You may even ask for help from some of them because going through a dead person's private possessions is a difficult job to do alone.

SELLING ITEMS OF VALUE

A family may well decide that the easiest way to sort out personal property is to sell everything and divide the money between them. If the deceased left a houseful of furniture and other personal effects, none of it of any particular value, the best thing is to call in some of the many second-hand dealers that advertise in the *Yellow Pages* and ask them what they will give to clear the whole house. It won't be much in most cases.

If you suspect that there are any items of value, though not amounting to enough to have to go to probate, it may be better to consult a saleroom. They can also be found in the *Yellow Pages* and they will send a representative around to the house to give a valuation of the item(s) in question.

KEEPING MEMENTOES

People like to keep little things to remember their dead friends and relations by and should, if possible, be given a chance to choose something of sentimental value. The most common thing people like to have as a reminder is something they bought the deceased as a gift at some time or another, probably because they put a lot of thought into buying it, it's something they like themselves, and it preserves a personal link.

It's common for children and younger people not to see any value in keeping things like these and then they come to regret the decision later. It's a good idea to put aside things for younger family members to give them later on special occasions such as coming of age, engagements or weddings. It's at times like these that they begin to appreciate a sense of family continuity and will be more likely to treasure something from the past.

SORTING OUT CLOTHES

Clothes can be ignored and left festering in wardrobes for years, but they are best sorted out and disposed of as soon as the next of kin can face up to it. The job can be difficult because it brings raw emotions to the surface but this can also help the process of grieving.

On a practical level, whoever is doing the job needs to take care because clothes are heavy and, once loaded into boxes or bags, can cause back injuries if they are lifted awkwardly.

There are several different ways to dispose of clothes:

- they can be thrown away

- they can be kept and worn by other members of the family

- they can be donated to charity shops or jumble sales

- they can be sold to second-hand dealers or at a car boot sale.

Throwing away
Normally, underwear that has been worn is thrown away, more from a sense of hygiene than anything else. But there is no hard and fast

rule about this and a fresh looking set of luxury silk undies may well find a home with someone else.

Charity shops and dealers won't accept underwear because of possible hygiene problems and because it can be distasteful to sort and store it.

If the next of kin don't like the thought of anyone else wearing any of the clothes of the deceased, or if the deceased didn't have anything worth keeping, everything can be put into plastic sacks or cardboard boxes and transported to the nearest tip. If no suitable transport is available, call the council waste disposal department to explain the circumstances and check that they will collect extra quantities, and leave it outside with the rubbish.

Wearing by other people

There are two schools of thought about this. Some people are superstitious about wearing the clothes of someone who has died. Some people don't like to wear second-hand clothes anyway and would find it doubly distasteful to wear the clothes of someone who has died.

Others find a lot of comfort in wearing the clothes of someone they loved who has died. They feel it keeps that person closer to them and is a kind of compliment to the deceased that they enjoy wearing the same clothes.

And some people simply need more clothes than they can afford to buy and are very glad to have the chance of something fresh to wear, wherever it has come from.

Selling

It may be that giving away clothes is a luxury a family can't afford. Though selling them won't raise a lot of money, there are times when every little helps, especially after the expense of a funeral.

There are always a number of second-hand dealers listed in the *Yellow Pages* and many of these will buy clothes as well as other items.

Clothes also go well in car boot sales if they are clean and attractively displayed. It's worth while trying to get hold of a special hanging rail so that people can browse more easily – clothes hanging up always look better than heaped on the ground or on a table.

Making donations to charity

Every town has a choice of charity shops that sell clothes and other second-hand items to raise funds. Most people will have their favourite charity and there will be little problem deciding which is to benefit from the clothes.

However, it is advisable to telephone first to check that the donation will be welcome because it does happen that some of these shops become over-stocked and have difficulty storing items. It's also a good idea to arrange with the shop when you'll be delivering the clothes because there isn't always someone there to accept them and put them into storage.

In addition, there is nearly always someone organising a jumble sale for some good cause or another and they will usually arrange collection from the house.

Once accepted by either charity shop or a jumble sale, the clothes will be of a double benefit because the charity will raise money and the person who buys them will get a bargain.

CHECKLIST

1. 'Personal chattels' are defined by law and should be valued as part of the estate of the deceased.

2. The deceased may have promised things to friends and family.

3. Even if nothing was promised, the family should be consulted before things are disposed of.

4. Personal mementoes are very important to some people.

5. Clothes and other items can be used to raise funds for charities.

CASE STUDIES

Jane thought carefully about her possessions

Jane gave her jewellery to Angela and also told her not to be afraid to look through her wardrobe and take anything she fancied. She sorted out the contents of her dressing table before she went into the hospice with her last illness and told Ralph that he was to take anything of value to the hospice charity shop and throw away the rest. Therefore when the time came he was able to get all her things sorted out, with Angela's help, secure in the knowledge that they were carrying out Jane's wishes.

Isabel faces another muddle

Isabel and Ralph lived in their farmhouse for 30 years and in that time threw nothing away. The first thing Isabel does is ask Ian if he wants anything of his father's and Ian chooses a couple of good tweed jackets, some shirts, and Alistair's fishing rods. Isabel sorts out the rest of the clothes and anything that seems worth keeping she puts to one side for Ian and Anna to take to a charity shop. The rest gets thrown away, including boxes and trunks of old photographs, old farm implements and other things that she just couldn't face sorting through. Later, after the house is sold, she regrets this and wishes she had kept more things from her early days with Alistair.

Jaswant's things are taken away

Jaswant's mother and her mother-in-law go to Ram's house and pack up all her clothes, then Ram calls in a second-hand dealer to take them away, and also the bed that Jaswant and Ram shared.

DISCUSSION POINTS

1. Would you be able to choose a memento from the possessions of a dear friend or relation who has died?

2. How long would you expect to have to wait before disposing of someone's personal effects?

3. Would you feel comfortable sorting through the personal possessions of someone who was close to you?

9
Grieving and Recovering

BEING LEFT ALONE

The funeral is over, the financial problems are being sorted out, the will is being dealt with, friends and family have gone and all that remains is a terrible feeling of emptiness and desolation as the bereaved person is finally left alone to face up to life without the one who has died.

It may be that the bereaved feels relief that it's all over, either because the deceased suffered a long and difficult illness or because the bereaved has long since tired of living with him or her for a number of reasons. This will almost certainly produce feelings of guilt which will be as difficult to deal with as grief.

Or the bereaved may be one of those people who feels nothing at all and is neither able to grieve nor feel relief.

The point is that people can have lots of different reactions to the death of someone close. All of them are normal but, because all human beings are different, everyone reacts in a different way.

GRIEVING NORMALLY

Some people think that grief is something to be kept private, others that it should be shared among a circle of close friends or family.

Many religions and cultures have strictly laid down rules about the grieving process and the support that must be given to the next of kin. In some ways this is helpful because everyone knows what to expect and what is expected of them. In other ways it can make things even worse for the next of kin when the formalities are over, the support is withdrawn and they are expected to get on with things.

Suffering strong reactions
It is more or less accepted nowadays that the bereaved of either sex

will cry at a funeral, though there are certainly people who still believe that crying isn't the done thing, especially for males, and are deeply embarrassed by any public show of grief.

What isn't realized is that the shock of a death can lead to the bereaved crying without warning in all sorts of situations – on a bus, at work, in a bank, on the telephone. This reaction can last for several weeks, if not months, and it usually results in the person who is crying apologising for their weakness and the person they are talking to wondering what they have said to trigger the tears.

In private the reaction can be stronger. Crying gives way to screaming and shouting and even throwing things and banging the walls and the furniture. Nothing is too dramatic and it is during these times that a person who has lost someone very close indeed often contemplates suicide.

There is also the phenomenon of the continuous 'action replay' of events before and after the death. The shocked brain seems to need to go over and over these events as though trying to convince itself that they are true, or as though trying to make them commonplace by repetition. The bereaved person has no control over these action replay sequences, they can occur at any time.

All this is perfectly normal and, however unlikely it seems at first, these reactions gradually become less frequent.

Analysing the grieving process

Nowadays it's recognised that getting over the grief of a bereavement successfully makes an important contribution to mental and emotional health, and even to physical health, later on in life. There have been many studies of the process of recovery.

This can be long and complicated or it can be brief and straightforward, according to the circumstances of the death, the background of the person suffering and their relationship to the deceased. It's generally recognised that there are several important stages to be gone through:

Shock
This produces many of the reactions described in Chapter 1. It can also include feelings of denial, that the doctors have made a mistake or that the events taking place are part of a dream. There is often a physical side to this shock, a feeling of tightness across the chest and throat so that breathing is difficult. There may be headaches, nausea, loss of appetite. In extreme cases shock causes physical illness to get a grip because the body's immune system can't cope.

Sorrow
This can be an overwhelming feeling of desolation on realising that the death must be accepted, that the dead person will never come back. It can also be mixed with almost irrational feelings of guilt that the death wouldn't have occurred if only . . . such and such had been done differently.

Anger
Sometimes this is quiet and inwardly directed. Sometimes, as mentioned above, it takes the form of screaming and shouting abuse – at the dead person for having the nerve to go, at God for letting such a thing happen, at oneself for caring so much, at anyone else who may be involved and especially at anyone who is trying to help.

Apathy and depression
Just at the time when friends think bereaved people should be beginning to get over their loss, it seems to get worse. They face the start of every day mourning the dead person and wondering if there is any point in getting out of bed. It's normal to lack interest in what is going on, to feel tired and, in extreme cases, to sink into clinical depression.

Recovery
This isn't just the appearance of a return to normality, because appearances can deceive. It's the stage when bereaved people begin to feel energy and enthusiasm for new projects, when they can go for whole days at a time without thinking about the person they have lost, and when they can remember and talk about the dead person without feelings of sorrow.

Reacting differently

It's important to understand that these are general descriptions of the most common progress through grief, but that doesn't mean that anyone with other symptoms and experiences is reacting abnormally. Some people don't appear to go through any of the stages, others find they are experiencing all of them at more or less the same time. And the stages don't necessarily occur in a neat progression, either – it's possible to move back and forth from one to another so that just when a person thinks they are getting used to their loss, all the old feelings come sweeping back.

Some people find that the pain eventually fades. Others find that it never goes away, they simply get used to living with it.

Some people get stuck in the angry or apathetic stages, or sink into clinical depression, and these people need special help.

SUFFERING IN SILENCE

One of the things that helps a person to make progress through their grief is talking about it. This is impossible for some people because the only person they had to talk to is now dead. And some people are too emotionally inhibited to open up and spill out their feelings to other people.

Also there are those who don't talk about their feelings because they are aware that there is a very real danger of boring and embarrassing their friends and neighbours. However hard people try to be sympathetic, sympathy soon wears thin and we all know the feeling of dread when we meet someone who constantly talks about themselves and their own troubles.

Suffering in silence isn't necessarily a bad course of action (or inaction), but friends and family can assume that it's a sign that everything is going fine, and the person is getting over their bereavement. In fact, the opposite may be true – the person may be feeling a lot of pain and be in need of more help than someone who screams and cries, or never stops talking.

HELPING OTHERS

The best form of help to give a friend who has suffered a bereavement is to understand what is going on for them and to be there to listen and offer companionship without being too intrusive.

Confronting the situation

Sometimes bereaved people find that friends cross the street to avoid them because they just don't know what to say and this causes a lot of extra pain. The best approach for someone who meets a bereaved friend for the first time after a death is to meet the situation head on. Walk up to them and say you are sorry to hear about whoever it is who has died.

Then normal conversation can resume according to the occasion or how well you know each other. You can carry on talking about the person who has died, and offer support, or you need never mention the matter again. But at least it has been brought into the open between you.

Listening

In the longer term, if a friend wants to talk about a bereavement, be there to listen. Avoid the temptation to do the talking and tell them all about your own bereavement, or about someone else you know who has been in a similar situation. Your friend will probably listen politely, but really doesn't want to hear all that. It won't help them to deal with their own grief.

Keeping in touch

Another useful thing to do, if you know a bereaved person who is now living alone, is to call in or telephone on a regular basis. Any excuse will do. You may also think it's a good idea to arrange some kind of outing, or ask your friend to join in with some group activity that you know about.

You will soon be able to gauge whether the contact is welcome or not and whether the person seems to be progressing back towards a normal life. If you suspect that they are not, that there are signs of depression or misery that seem to be getting them down, you could suggest asking for help from a befriending group or a bereavement counsellor (see next section).

GETTING HELP FOR YOURSELF

The bereaved person who has good friends to keep an eye on them and look after their welfare is lucky. Many people are forced to suffer alone, or to keep a job and family going without showing too much pain, which can be just as lonely as never seeing another person.

Being unable to cope

A feeling of being unable to cope with the grieving process can be as hard to overcome as the grief itself. Signs to look out for are:

- inability to sleep, however tired you are

- lack of appetite for food

- lack of interest in home and family

- poor concentration

- a tendency to have accidents

- shortness of temper with members of your family

- physical aggression towards other people

- reliance on alcohol or other drugs (whether legally or illegally obtained).

Recognising that you are not coping and that this is more than just a temporary phase is only half the battle. You then need to convince yourself that you will be taken seriously if you seek help.

Asking for help
For many people the obvious place to go for help is the doctor's surgery.

Many GPs are sympathetic towards people suffering in this way and will take time and trouble to get to the root of the problem. They will be able to sign a person off work so that there is a chance to recover, freed from some of their burden. A lot of GPs' surgeries also have a practice counsellor who can offer special help.

Unfortunately there are some doctors who are neither sympathetic nor knowledgeable about grief and will prescribe a few sleeping tablets in the hope that the problem will solve itself.

One organisation which can offer both short and long-term help is Cruse Bereavement Care, a national charity founded initially to help widows and their children but now offering free professional counselling to all bereaved people who ask for it, and support groups for those whose need is simply to get out of the house and talk to someone. Bereavement counselling services are also offered by some funeral directors.

Understanding counselling
Many people in need of counselling avoid asking for help because of a misunderstanding of what counselling is about. They see it as 'busybody' activity, or as someone coming round to try to talk them out of their depressed state and advise them on how to run their lives.

This is a long way from the truth. A counsellor, in whatever specialism, is trained to listen, not to talk. The last thing a competent counsellor will ever do is try to tell a client what they should or should not be doing. He or she is there to help people to unbottle their fears and miseries in a safe situation and come to terms with whatever is causing problems.

A bereavement counsellor is particularly knowledgeable about the processes of recovering from the death of someone close and is trained to recognise when someone has got stuck on the road to recovery.

Asking for this kind of help is not an admission of weakness, it is a sensible move towards self-preservation and will help you on your way to getting on with your life.

REMEMBERING GRIEVING CHILDREN

Children are often the forgotten mourners in the turmoil of a family bereavement. They can be pushed aside as other matters, which seem more important at the time, have to be dealt with. Often they are sent away, or farmed out to neighbours, because they can't be looked after properly by the family. And many people don't think that children should attend funerals, which shuts off part of the formal grieving process for them.

A child who has suffered the loss of someone dear to them feels it very deeply indeed. Bereavement usually goes hand in hand with a terrifying sense of insecurity and the feeling that, if one person has died, it can happen to the rest of the family too.

However bad the adults feel, it's important that time is taken to talk to the children, to listen to their fears and grief, and to reassure them. They may appear to be coping well on the surface but symptoms of serious reactions may show up as bed-wetting, nightmares, tantrums or disruptive behaviour at school.

All this should be treated with understanding and if the family can't deal with the child's problems themselves, help can be found through a school counsellor, or through Cruse Bereavement Care who have counsellors specialising in children's problems.

STARTING A NEW LIFE

Carrying on as before
Some people getting over a bereavement just want to be able to get on with their life the way it was before, minus the person who has died, even though they know that it can never be quite the same again.

These people will make efforts to carry on with their friendships and activities and in many ways, surrounded by the familiar and the predictable, will find the road to recovery relatively smooth.

Making a new start

Some people will find it very difficult to try to fit into the old patterns. They will find that simply being without the person who has died closes doors. For example:

- The loss of a child can separate the bereaved from the company of the parents of that child's friends, or from groups that revolved around school or youth club. Even having to drop out of the 'school run' can cut off a large part of some people's social lives.

- The loss of a parent or a partner can make it difficult to carry on with hobbies or holiday activities that were shared.

- The loss of a partner can catapult a person back into the lifestyle of a single person. Friends may say that it doesn't matter to them whether a person is single or part of a couple but it's surprising how many of them don't invite the single person out any more, and surprising how difficult it is for the bereaved person to go to events where everyone seems to be part of a couple.

And any of the above losses can lead to the bereaved wanting to avoid going to certain places that bring back memories of the dead person.

Some people deal with these situations by getting a new job and/or moving house to a new part of the country. If such radical changes are not possible, taking up a new hobby or joining a new activity group can bring a fresh circle of friends and acquaintances.

Finding a new partner

In some cases people who have been bereaved of their partners look for a new partner quite quickly, both to ease their loneliness and to help with the problems of bringing up a family alone.

There is no doubt that for some people this works well. Mistakes to avoid are:

- expecting the new partner to resemble the dead one

- expecting the new relationship to be the same as the old one

- not being honest with your reasons for starting up the new relationship

- constantly talking about the person who has died

- if the new partner is also a bereaved person, resenting it if they talk about their dead partner.

Whatever a bereaved person does to try to rebuild a life after their loss, they will need all the help they can get from friends and family. The remarkable thing is that, every year, thousands of people do succeed in coming to terms with bereavement and, however much they have been affected, learning to live again.

CHECKLIST

1. Grieving is a long process with several stages to go through.

2. Grieving people often experience very strong reactions.

3. Try not to avoid a person who has been bereaved.

4. Try not to let a bereaved person suffer in silence.

5. There is specialist help for bereaved people who can't recover on their own.

6. Most people do manage to start a new life eventually.

CASE STUDIES

Ralph finds himself in trouble

Ralph finds the gap left by Jane agonising. His sons have gone back to their own lives and Angela is preoccupied with her examinations, so he has a lot of time on his own. He wakes up in the mornings after a fitful night's sleep with a tightness in his chest and often finds himself weeping as he makes the morning tea. He tries to continue playing golf and attending his local camera club, but finds the sympathy of his fellow club members upsets him too much. He tries getting himself to sleep by drinking whisky in the evening but that only makes him feel more miserable.

He has a leaflet from Cruse Bereavement Care in a pack that he was given at the hospice but he ignored it, thinking he wouldn't need that sort of help. Eventually he swallows his pride and telephones Cruse, and asks for a counsellor to visit him. Gradually the burden lifts and he is able to resume his golfing and photography.

Isabel makes a new life

Once the farm is sold Isabel moves into a small bungalow in the nearby village and quickly makes friends through the church and the Women's Institute. Stuck on the farm, helping Alistair, she had never had much of a social life and she begins to realise what she has missed out on. When winter comes she joins an art class and a cookery class. She is soon so busy that she hardly has time to see Ian and Anna. She certainly hardly misses Alistair and is secretly but guiltily grateful that he died when he did instead of dragging on, becoming more and more sick and disorientated.

Ram has 40 days

For 40 days Ram Singh isn't expected to attend the temple or take part in any social events. He doesn't even have to go to work, but as this isn't forbidden and the business needs his attention, he starts again a week after the final prayers of Jaswant's funeral. His mother helps him to care for the children and he tries to fill the gap in their lives by leaving the shop early to help them with their homework and be with them in the evenings.

After a month has passed the members of the management committee of the temple visit Ram to inquire about the well-being of him and his family, and to ask them to come to the temple. Ram puts this off because he never was a good attender, but eventually he does go to prayers and finds that the solidarity of the community makes him feel less lonely. About a year after Jaswant's death his mother begins to hint that he should look for another wife to take care of his children.

DISCUSSION POINTS

1. Do you want to show sympathy for a bereaved friend but don't know what to say?

2. Do you suspect that someone you know isn't recovering from their grief? How can you help without intruding?

3. Do you know someone who is trying to get on with their life after a bereavement? What are they finding most difficult?

4. Have you ever been shocked to see someone appearing to enjoy life on their own soon after a bereavement?

10
Anticipating Your Own Death

TALKING ABOUT DYING

There is no tradition in Britain of preparing for our own death. People who do try to do this, or who try to talk to their friends and families about it, are considered indelicate, out of order, sometimes downright morbid. According to the Law Society, only about a third of us even write a will.

Considering the problems that this lack of foresight can cause for the people who are left behind to deal with the aftermath of a death, this is a strange state of affairs. Just think of how much easier it will be for those who are bereaved by your death if their pain isn't complicated by financial problems and the need to make serious decisions about where you die, how to conduct your funeral and the disposal of your property.

Just think how much better they will feel if they know that all the arrangements have been made and the bills have been met because you took the trouble to spare them all the extra stress.

Making your own arrangements
Recently there have been moves from several different groups towards encouraging people to plan for their own deaths and funerals. For example:

- The Law Society is always trying to encourage people to make wills.

- The Natural Death Centre has proposed a Declaration of Rights for the Person Dying at Home and also provides an outline suggestion for writing 'advanced funeral wishes'.

- Several groups have suggested that people write a 'living will' containing instructions as to how they would like to be treated (including medical treatment) when they are dying.

- Age Concern first encouraged pre-paid funeral plans, now available from several insurance companies and funeral directors.

- Age Concern also publishes a pack for giving instructions to your next of kin about what arrangements you have made and where all the relevant documents can be found in the event of your death.

- The Catholic Church advises people who want to be cremated (which Catholics were once forbidden to do) to write a letter leaving instructions about this so that their priest is in no doubt.

- The National Funerals College has written a consultative document, the *Dead Citizen's Charter*, in an effort to improve the quality of funerals and people's understanding of their rights.

With all this encouragement it may not be long before it's the normal thing to plan for your own death and talk it over with your family.

WRITING YOUR WILL

Dividing up your property
Even someone who doesn't have very much property can write a will to make sure that the little they have goes to the people they want to have it. Without a will this may not happen because, as was explained earlier, the property of an intestate person has to be divided up according to the law.

Getting the wording right
The Law Society advises people to go to a solicitor to have a will drawn up and it is true that if you do this you can be sure that the wording will be correct and there won't be any loopholes.

At the time of writing (1996) the cost should be around £50–£60 unless there are a lot of complications.

However, it isn't compulsory to employ a solicitor to do the job. You can start with a blank piece of paper and do it all yourself or with the help of a handbook such as the Which? publication *Make Your Own Will* (applicable to England and Wales only).

You can also buy will and testament forms in any well-stocked stationery shop, including the post office, which set out the correct wording and give instructions about the witnessing procedures – however, be careful to follow the instructions carefully or you may end up with a will that is at best difficult to interpret, at worst invalid (Figure 10).

Providing for dependant children

Wills aren't only about leaving money. You can also appoint someone to be guardian to any dependant children you may leave behind you, if they haven't another parent to do the job. It's as well to ask the person beforehand because they would be able to refuse. It's also sensible to arrange any money or insurance policies you have so that there will be something available to provide for them.

If you don't make provision in your will for dependant children the person who is left to look after them can challenge the will so that they are provided for.

Providing for animals

Pet animals often get forgotten in all the arrangements that have to be made, yet they can suffer just as much as humans over a bereavement – sometimes more so, because some families take the easy way out and have a pet destroyed when an elderly owner dies.

The very least a pet owner can do is make arrangements with friends or relatives for the care of pets in the event of their death. However, it is possible to go further and to make arrangements with the Cinnamon Trust, the Blue Cross or the Cats' Protection League (cats only) to care for bereaved pets. These organisations will all look after and try to rehome the animals. Ideally they appreciate prior arrangements being made, and some help towards expenses by way of a donation or legacy, though money isn't necessary for them to take action on behalf of a pet in need.

Appointing an executor

An executor can be a solicitor, a business colleague or a trusted friend or relative who will do the necessary work after you have gone. As explained in Chapter 7, this isn't impossibly difficult but it can be tedious and can cost money. Because of this it's customary to ask someone if they are willing to do the job for you before you name them, and also to leave them something in the will.

There is no legal requirement to name an executor at all. You can just leave it to whoever is willing to volunteer when the time comes – or whoever is most desperate to get their hands on your money!

<u>THIS IS THE LAST WILL</u> of me <u>RALPH SANDERS</u>

of 2, The Green, Anytown, United Kingdom.

1. <u>I REVOKE</u> all former Wills and Testamentary dispositions made by me.

2. <u>I APPOINT</u> the partners at the date of my death of the firm Smith & Jones of Anytown, to be my executors and trustee and I wish that two of them shall prove my will and act initially in its trusts.

3. <u>I GIVE</u> my executors the absolute power to call in and convert my ready money and all parts of my estate and after payment therefrom of my debts and funeral expenses and testamentary expenses, to divide all my remaining estate in equal shares between my three children, John Sanders, Peter Sanders and Angela Sanders.

4. <u>IF ANY</u> of the above-named children should have died in my lifetime, their surviving child or children shall take, and if more than one in equal shares absolutely, the share which his or her parent would have taken had he or she survived <u>BUT</u> if any of my children should have died in my lifetime and left no issue, my remaining children to take equal shares of my estate.

<u>IN WITNESS</u> whereof I have hereunto set my hand this Second day of January One Thousand, Nine Hundred and Ninety Six.

<u>SIGNED</u> by the said <u>RALPH SANDERS</u> in   *Ralph Sanders.*

our presence and then by us in his:-

<u>FIRST WITNESS</u>   <u>SECOND WITNESS</u>

Jane Brown   William Brown
4 THE GREEN   4 THE GREEN
ANYTOWN   ANYTOWN

Fig. 10. Ralph Sanders' will.
(In Scotland the two witnesses would not be legally necessary.)

LIVING WILL OF RALPH SANDERS OF 2, The Green, Anytown.

1. If at all possible I wish my death to take place in hospital or hospice so as not to place the expectation of my care on my sons and daughter or their spouses or children.

2. If I am suffering from a terminal illness and unable to make my own decisions I do not want any medication or treatment that may prolong my life artificially.

3. If I am suffering from any injury that makes me unable to make decisions and from which I can't recover I do not want any treatment that would prolong my life, including force feeding or a life-support machine.

4. If the illness or injury from which I am suffering is painful I would like pain-killers to be administered even if this makes me comatose.

5. I would like my friends and family to be able to say goodbye to me without feeling that they must stay around after I am unable to speak to or recognise them. On the other hand, if they will feel better to be with me at the end, I give my consent for them to be with me.

6. I want to make sure that my dog Rover, or any other animal I own at the time of my death, will go to the home of one of my children. If this isn't immediately possible the animal or animals to be taken care of by the Blue Cross until a home can be arranged, and my children to make a substantial donation to pay for the care.

7. My funeral to be conducted in accordance with the plan lodged with James Black, Funeral Director of Anytown.

Ralph Sanders.   1st Jan. '9X

Fig. 11. Ralph Sanders' living will.

WRITING A 'LIVING WILL'

Leaving it too late

When people are nearing death it is often too late to begin to give instructions about the way they want to be treated.

For example, someone who has suffered a stroke, or someone with multiple sclerosis, Alzheimer's, cancer, AIDS, CJD, may spend their last weeks or months unfit to make any decisions because of senility or because they are comatose from injury or pain-killers. Or someone who has been involved in an accident may be on a life-support machine and unable to communicate with those around them.

Considering the end

The idea of a living will is that you can relieve your next of kin, or the medical staff attending you, of difficult decisions. For example:

- How long they should continue to try to prolong your life by force feeding or medical treatment.

- Whether you would rather be relieved of pain even though it will make you incapable of communicating with them any more.

- Whether you want to remain conscious even if it means your death may be painful.

- Whether a life-support machine should continue to be used for you if you are technically brain dead.

You can also state whether, if there is a choice, you would rather die at home or in a hospital or hospice, whether you want friends and family to visit you or not, what kind of religious attendance you want. And you can write detailed instructions for your funeral.

Discussing euthanasia

What you should not try to do is express any wishes about euthanasia because no doctor or nurse can follow these wishes. The arguments for and against euthanasia are complex and there is nothing to stop anyone discussing them with friends and family but it must be remembered that the law is quite clear about it at present. Euthanasia is a crime and anyone you ask to help you, even if you call it 'assisted suicide', will be in danger of being prosecuted and going to prison.

Putting it down on paper

You will find suggestions and guidelines about writing a living will from the Natural Death Centre, and it's suggested in different forms in several of the publications listed in the Further Reading section of this book. Age Concern issues a form for giving instructions after your death, but it doesn't include anything about treatment whilst dying.

However, because a living will isn't a legal document, the ideas it contains are more important than the wording. Its contents aren't legally enforceable in the same way as a traditional will, but the guidelines you set down may be useful to those who will one day have to make decisions on your behalf. As long as they are reasonable guidelines and as long as circumstances permit, the people around you should do their best to follow them (Figure 11).

ARRANGING YOUR OWN FUNERAL

Your living will can give outline instructions for your funeral or can even contain a complete funeral plan, either through a funeral director or for an independent funeral.

Pre-paying your own funeral

You can go to one of the insurance companies or funeral directors that arranges pre-paid funerals and fill in one of their forms, make the necessary payments, and do no more. Or you can take out one of these funeral plans and add to it certain ideas about the readings and music you want.

The benefits are:

• You will be buying tomorrow's funeral at today's prices, which could increase ten-fold if you live another 25 years.

• You will know that your relatives won't have to worry about a funeral bill they may have difficulty in paying.

Leaving instructions for an independent funeral

It's also possible to make detailed arrangements for a funeral without a funeral director, though it would be a good idea to talk over these arrangements with the people who are going to have to do the job.

The sort of things you need to think about are:

- Making sure that someone will be available to attend to the laying out of your body.

- Buying or making your own coffin and storing it somewhere safe.

- Buying your plot of land in a cemetery or woodland burial site, or making pre-paid arrangements with a crematorium.

- If you are to be cremated, giving specific instructions about the disposal of your ashes.

- Selecting the readings and music for your funeral (writing your own if you want to).

- Arranging who you want to officiate at the funeral.

- Giving instructions about flowers and notices in the newspaper.

- Giving instructions about the kind of memorial you would like, if any.

- Writing a list of who you want to be informed of your death and to attend your funeral.

- Making arrangements for the post-funeral refreshments.

INFORMING OTHER PEOPLE

The final thing you need to think about is telling people that you have done all this and where they can find it in writing. It's no use writing a living will giving instructions about your death if nobody will go through your papers until after you have gone.

Much better to give copies of it to several relatives or friends who you expect to be interested in your death. At first they may try to tell you they don't want to think about it and a little insistence may be necessary to get your message across. You can also give copies to your doctor, bank manager and solicitor.

On the other hand, you may be part of a circle of like-minded people who will make plans together, exchange instructions, and see them for the good idea they are. The chances are that you will actually have quite a lot of fun doing this. And without doubt the surviving members of your family will bless you for it.

CHECKLIST

1. Don't be afraid to talk about dying.

2. Don't be afraid to ask questions and find out about your rights before and after your death.

3. Don't avoid writing a will: you may leave more behind you than you think.

4. Make sure your will is correctly worded and witnessed.

5. Writing a 'living will' can relieve the people caring for you of difficult decisions.

6. Think about making provision for the care of your children. . .

7. . . . and of your pets.

8. Planning your own funeral can be a positive exercise.

CASE STUDIES

Ralph reviews his plans

Ralph made his living will and funeral plans at the same time as Jane did. After her death he reviews all his plans, and rewrites his will to make his children and his possible future grandchildren his beneficiaries. The only other thing to do is to tell his three children what he has done, and where all the relevant papers are. He also tries to encourage them to do the same even though they are still young.

Isabel makes a will

After finding Alistair's affairs in such a muddle, Isabel decides to do things properly. She visits a solicitor to have a will drawn up, leaving everything to Ian. She also uses some of her spare cash to take out a pre-paid funeral plan and leaves instructions with her solicitor and bank manager.

Ram thinks about his children

Although Ram knows that his children will be looked after by his family if he dies before they are grown up, he decides to make certain of their future because the business belongs to his whole family and there are certain outstanding mortgages. He takes out a life insurance policy which is written in trust for his two children, then goes to a solicitor he knows and has a will written which leaves the children everything he owns in equal shares. The solicitor reminds him that if he remarries he will have to write another will as the current one will become invalid.

DISCUSSION POINTS

1. How can you convince people that it makes good sense to discuss and plan for their own death?

2. Why are the wording and witnessing of a will important?

3. What sort of things would you include in a living will?

4. What would you do if you found a living will belonging to a member of your family who was dying?

5. Have you thought about planning your own funeral?

Discussion Points: Suggested Solutions

CHAPTER 1

1. There is no easy way to do this. If you think you are closest to the dying person, don't leave it to other people. But try to talk it over with someone else first, and have them with you when you bring up the subject. Don't beat about the bush. Try something like 'Can we talk about how much longer do you think you are going to be with us?'.

2. Talk to the patient, the doctors, the nurses and the other carers. Remember, the patient's rights are more important than the feelings of the medical staff. If necessary, move the patient somewhere else.

3. This can clear up a lot of misunderstandings.

4. Speak to people, gently. Explain that the patient is tired and suggest other ways they can be supportive.

5. Try your friends and family, the Macmillan and Marie Curie Services, your nearest hospice. They are all there to help.

CHAPTER 2

1. The police are only doing their job. Ask as many questions as you want to and try to be helpful.

2. If not, ask them. And tell them about your wishes for your own body.

3. Ask the Coroner's Office, or the Procurator Fiscal's Office. Or if you have a solicitor acting for you, ask him or her to find out.

4. Ask for a Judicial Review. But best to consult a solicitor first.

CHAPTER 3

1. The only essential paper is the Cause of Death Certificate from a doctor or the office of a Coroner, or a Sheriff in Scotland. It is helpful to take such things as birth and marriage certificates if you can find them.

2. The identity of the deceased and the cause of the death.

3. If the registrar is suspicious that the cause of death isn't what is written on the certificate, the Coroner will be informed.

CHAPTER 4

1. Why not ask them? And tell them what you want.

2. Why not ask a funeral director, a crematorium director or a cemetery superintendent? They are usually more than happy to show people around and answer questions.

3. This isn't easy and often you just can't please everyone. The closest family are the most important. Make a list of possible dates and go for the one that's easiest for most people, then book it with the funeral director or the other authorities.

CHAPTER 5

1. There are a lot of details to attend to and a list needs to be made of what these are and in what order you should tackle them. Don't forget that money will be needed to pre-pay for many of the arrangements.

2. If you are at all worried about this task you can ask for help from a district nurse or a funeral director.

3. There are several organisations which will give you advice but the first people you can turn to are the burial ground or crematorium authorities.

CHAPTER 6

1. They have to make sure that the money left in the deceased customer's accounts goes to the people who are entitled to it by law, after payment of funeral expenses and probate fees.

2. If you haven't already made arrangements to have access to money of your own, it's a good idea to do something about it before it's too late.

3. There are a lot of ways to cut down on spending and a funeral doesn't have to be lavish to show respect. If there isn't enough money for even the most basic funeral an approach can be made to the Benefits Office or your local authority.

CHAPTER 7

1. An executor's first duty is to deal with the financial affairs of the deceased. In reality this may also mean arranging a funeral and applying for Probate or Confirmation.

2. Grant of Probate (England, Wales and Northern Ireland) or Letters of Confirmation (Scotland) establish the right of the applicant to deal with the financial affairs of the deceased. It also confirms the legality of the will, if there is one.

3. Usually there will be evidence amongst the papers of the deceased. An advertisement should be put in the local paper, and can be put in the *London Gazette*.

4. This would be a good idea if you were in any doubt about how to go about your duties, because you are legally and financially responsible for any mistakes, and solicitors are insured against that sort of thing.

CHAPTER 8

1. It's nice to have the chance to keep something of sentimental value but not easy to decide on what.

2. It depends on the value of the person's estate. Legally the executor should wait six months to allow all creditors a chance to make

claims. However, many people sort out personal effects as soon as they are reasonably certain there will be no claims.

3. This is never an easy thing to do but it can be an important part of the grieving process and it is better done by someone close to the deceased than by a stranger.

CHAPTER 9

1. Don't avoid the issue. Tell the truth, say you are sorry about what's happened.

2. Be around, listen, suggest going out, suggest talking to a bereavement counsellor. Whatever you do, don't give up on them.

3. There are so many things that are difficult that they probably don't know themselves which is the biggest problem. Don't make things worse by ignoring them or trying to tell them what they should be doing.

4. You may be shocked but it's up to them to live their lives the way they see best.

CHAPTER 10

1. The best way to convince someone is to ask them how they would feel if they were left to cope with everything for another member of their family.

2. If a mistake is made in the wording process the estate might not go the people you intend. If the witnessing is done incorrectly it can make the will invalid.

3. All your wishes about how you would like to be treated during your last illness, and how you would like your funeral and memorial to be arranged.

4. The best thing would be to read it, show it to other people concerned in the care of the dying person, and try to stick to what it says.

5. Why not start now?

Glossary

Annuity. A sum of money paid at regular intervals to a person who has invested a capital sum with an insurance company for this purpose.

Ashes. The remains of a body after cremation, correctly known as the cremated remains.

Autopsy. An examination of a body by a pathologist, to find out the cause of death (also known as a *post mortem*).

Beneficiary. Anyone who will benefit from a dead person's estate.

Bereavement. Loss by death of a person you know.

Bond of caution. (Cay-shun) a bond taken out in Scotland through an individual or an insurance company to protect an executor against claims if a mistake is made in administration of an estate.

Carer. One who takes care of another person when they are unable to look after themselves.

Certificate of Cause of Death. The certificate issued by an attending doctor, or the Coroner, that has to be taken to the Registrar.

Certificate for Burial or Cremation. A form, known as the Green Form, issued by the Registrar authorising a funeral to take place.

Confirmation. The authorisation issued in Scotland by the Commissary Office to allow an applicant to take control of a dead person's assets (equivalent of a Grant of Probate).

Coroner. An officer appointed to investigate sudden or unexplained deaths in England, Wales and Northern Ireland.

Creditor. A person who is owed money.

Cremated remains. The remains of a body after a cremation (also referred to as the ashes).

Death Certificate. A copy of the entry in the Register of Deaths, used to prove death when necessary.

Deceased. A person who has died.

Estate. Everything owned by a person up to the date of death.

Executor. A person appointed either by the deceased or by a court to deal with the financial affairs of a dead person and administer their estate.

Executor dative. In Scotland, a person appointed as executor by a court if the deceased didn't appoint an executor.

Hospice. A special hospital where terminally ill patients can go to receive palliative care (that relieves pain but does not necessarily prolong life).

Informant. A person entitled to give information about a death to the Registrar.

Inquest. An inquiry into the cause of a sudden or unexplained death, conducted by a Coroner.

Intestacy. Dying without making a will.

Living will. A document specifying how a person wishes to be treated while they are dying, and how they wish their funeral to be arranged. This is not legally binding.

Neo natal death. Death of an infant within 28 days of birth.

Next of kin. The nearest relative by blood or marriage to a dead person.

Officiant. The person who leads a funeral service.

Palliative care. Medical care that improves the quality of a patient's life but doesn't seek to cure or to prolong life.

Pathologist. A medical specialist who examines dead bodies for evidence of cause of death. A consultant pathologist is attached to a hospital and a forensic pathologist works for the Home Office.

Personal chattels. A legally defined list of possessions that a person can leave as part of their estate (also known as personal effects).

Post mortem. An examination of a body by a pathologist (also known as an autopsy).

Probate (Grant of). A document issued by the Probate Office authorising an applicant to take control of a dead person's assets and administer them.

Procurator Fiscal. An investigating officer who is the Scottish equivalent to a Coroner.

Registrar. The officer responsible for registering births, marriages and deaths.

Stillbirth. Birth of a dead baby after the 24th week of pregnancy.

Will (or Testament). A legal document directing how a person's property is to be disposed of after their death.

Useful Reading

CHAPTER 1

Cicely Saunders – The Founder of the Modern Hospice Movement, Biography, Shirley du Boulay (Hodder & Stoughton, 1984, 1994).

Living with Dying, Helen Alexander (ed) (Broadcasting Support Services, 1990).

I Don't Know What to Say, Dr Robert Buckman (Macmillan & Papermac, 1988, 1990).

Coping With a Dying Relative, Derek Doyle (MacDonald, Edinburgh 1983).

CHAPTER 3

What to Do When Someone Dies, Paul Harris (Consumers Association, 1994).

What to Do After a Death in England and Wales, Benefits Agency D49 (HMSO, 1995).

What to Do After a Death in Scotland, The Scottish Office Home Department.

CHAPTER 4

Funerals and How to Improve Them, Dr Tony Walter (Hodder & Stoughton, 1990).

The Dead Citizen's Charter, National Funerals College (1996).

CHAPTER 5

The Natural Death Handbook, Nicholas Albery, Gil Elliot and Joseph Elliot (eds) (Virgin Books, 1993).

Before and After, Natural Death Centre Awards, Nicholas Albery, Matthew Mezey, Mary McHugh and Marie Papworth (eds) (Natural Death Centre, 1995).

Funerals Without God, Jane Wynne Willson (British Humanist Association, 1989, 1995).

CHAPTER 6

Widows' Benefits, Benefits Agency NP45 (HMSO, 1996).
A Guide to the Social Fund, Benefits Agency SB16 (HMSO, 1996).
What to Do after a Death in Scotland: Social Security Supplement D49S (HMSO, 1995).

CHAPTER 7

A Step by Step Guide to Wills & Probate, AK Biggs & K Donelly (Callow Publishing, 1991, 1994) – England and Wales only.

CHAPTER 9

Losing a Parent, Fiona Marshall (Sheldon Press, SPCK, 1993).

CHAPTER 10

Let Me Decide, Dr William Molloy and Virginia Mepham (Penguin).
Make Your Own Will, Which? Action Pack (Consumer's Association & Penguin) – England and Wales only.
Making a Will Won't Kill You, The Law Society.
Putting Your Affairs in Order, Age Concern.
The Which? Guide to Giving and Inheriting, Jonquil Lowe (Consumers Association, 1992, 1996).

Useful Addresses

CARE FOR THE DYING

Hospice Information Service, 51–59 Lawrie Park Road, Sydenham, London SE26 6DZ. Tel: (0181) 778 9252.

Macmillan Cancer Relief Fund, Anchor House, 15–19 Britten Street, London SE3 3TZ. Tel: (0171) 351 7811.

Marie Curie Cancer Care, 28 Belgrave Square, London SW1X 8QG. Tel: (0171) 235 3325.

Terrence Higgins Trust, 52–54 Grays Inn Road, London WC1X 8JU. Tel: (0171) 242 1010.

ARRANGING FUNERALS

British Humanist Association, 47 Theobald's Road, London WC1X 8SP. Tel: (0171) 430 0908.

Carlisle City Council, Bereavement Services, Richardson Street, Carlisle CA2 6AL. Tel: (01228) 25022.

Compakta Limited, 2 Newbold Road, Desford, Leicestershire LE9 9GS. Tel: (01455) 828642.

Green Undertakings, 1 Williton High Street, Somerset TA4 4NW. Tel: (01984) 632285.

Heaven on Earth, 47 Picton Street, Montpelier, Bristol BS6 5PZ. Tel: (0117) 942 1836.

Humanist Society of Scotland, 17 Howburn Place, Aberdeen AB1 2XT. Tel: (01224) 573034.

National Association of Funeral Directors, 618 Warwick Road, Solihull, West Midlands B91 1AA. Tel: (0121) 711 1343.

Peace Burials, St Peter's Villa, Ridley Lane, Mawdesley, Lancashire L40 3SX. Tel: (01704) 821900.

The Funeral Ombudsman, 31 Southampton Row, London WC1B 5JH. Tel: (0171) 430 1112.

The Funeral Centre, 43–47 Rushey Green, Catford, London SE6 4AS. Tel: (0181) 695 0999.

The Natural Death Centre, 20 Heber Road, London NW2 6AA. Tel: (0181) 208 2853.

BURIALS AT SEA

Agriculture and Fisheries Department (Scotland), Marine Laboratory, PO Box 101, Victoria Road, Aberdeen AB9 8DB. Tel: (01224) 876544.

Ministry of Agriculture, Fisheries and Food (England and Wales), Environmental Protection Division, Nobel House, 17 Smith Square, London SW1P 3JR. Tel: (0171) 238 6000.

The Britannia Shipping Company for Burial at Sea Ltd, Britannia House, Newton Poppleford, Sidmouth, Devon EX10 0EF. Tel: (01395) 568652.

DEALING WITH A WILL

Principal Probate Registry, Somerset House, Strand, London WC2R 1LP. Tel: (0171) 936 6983/7464.

The Commissary Office, 16 North Bank Street, Edinburgh EH1 2NS. Tel: (0131) 225 2525 Ext 2253.

The Master, Probate and Matrimonial Office, Royal Courts of Justice (Northern Ireland), PO Box 410, Chichester Street, Belfast BT1 3JE. Tel: (01232) 235111.

SOCIAL SECURITY PUBLICATIONS

HMSO, The Causeway, Oldham Broadway Business Park, Chadderton, Oldham OL9 9XD.

The Scottish Office Home Department, St Andrew's House, Edinburgh EH1 3DG. Tel: (0131) 244 3458.

TAXATION

Inland Revenue (England and Wales), Capital Taxes Office, Ferrers House, PO Box 38, Castle Meadow Road, Nottingham NG2 1BB. Tel: (0115) 974 2400.

Inland Revenue (Scotland), Capital Taxes Office, Mulberry House, 16 Picardy Place, Edinburgh EH1 3NB. Tel: (0131) 556 8511.

Inland Revenue (N. Ireland), Capital Taxes Office, Level 3, Dorchester House, 52–58 Great Victoria Street, Belfast BT2 7QL. Tel: (01232) 315556 Ext 2337.

BEREAVEMENT

Cruse Bereavement Care, Cruse House, 126 Sheen Road,
Richmond, Surrey TW9 1UR. Tel: (0181) 940 4818.
and
18 South Trinity Road, Edinburgh EH5 3PN. Tel: (0131) 551
1511.
The Stillbirth and Neonatal Death Society, 28 Portland Place, London
W1N 4DE. Tel: (0171) 436 5881.

PLANNING AHEAD

Age Concern (England), Astral House, 1268 London Road, London
SW16 4ER. Tel: (0181) 679 8000.
Age Concern (Scotland), 54a Fountainbridge, Edinburgh EH3 9PT.
Tel: (0131) 228 5656.
Age Concern (Wales), 4th Floor, 1 Cathedral Road, Cardiff. Tel:
(01222) 371566.
British Organ Donor Society, Balsham, Cambridge CB1 6DL. Tel:
(01223) 893636.
Chosen Heritage, Funeral Plans Ltd, Farringdon House, Wood Street,
East Grinstead, West Sussex RH19 1EW. Tel: 0800 525555.
The Law Society, 113 Chancery Lane, London WC2A 1PL. Tel: (0171)
242 1222.
Voluntary Euthanasia Society, 13 Prince of Wales Terrace, London
W8 5PG. Tel: (0171) 937 7770.

CARE OF ANIMALS

Blue Cross, Shilton Road, Burford, Oxon OX18 4PF. Tel: (01993)
822483.
The Cats Protection League, 17 Kings Road, Horsham, West Sussex
RH13 5PN. Tel: (01403) 261947.
The Cinnamon Trust, Foundry House, Foundry Square, Hayle,
Cornwall TR27 4HH. Tel: (01326) 574493.

Index